RISE ABOVE THE RUT

REDISCOVERING JOY AND PURPOSE IN YOUR LIFE

JAY NESBIT

ONE BOOKS

ONE BOOKS PUBLISHING
One University Circle – Suite 1402
Cleveland, OH 44106
onebookspublishing@gmail.com

Cover and Interior Design by Vanessa Mendozzi
Website Design by Kiersten Armstrong
First Editing by Dr. Michael

Rise Above the Rut: Rediscovering Joy and Purpose in Your Life

Paperback ISBN: 979-8-9884949-1-1
eBook ISBN: 979-8-9884949-0-4

Library of Congress Control Number: 2023913072

www.jaynesbit.com

Printed in the United States of America

This book is dedicated to all of you who have faced challenges and struggled to learn, grow, or live the life of your dreams.

May this book empower and inspire you to create new realities and embark on a remarkable journey of achievement.

A whopping 92% of people who set New Year's goals never actually achieve them.[1]

Only around 25% of American adults say they have a clear sense of what makes their lives meaningful.[2]

No matter how long you have traveled in the wrong direction, you can always turn around.[3]

---

1 Joseph Luciani, *Journal of Clinical Psychology*, 2015.

2 Dhruv Khullar, *The New York Times*, 2018.

3 Anonymous Author.

Get ready for an incredible journey that will bring a deeper sense of meaning to your life.

This book is packed with life-changing skills and practical tools to unlock your full potential. It guides you to break free from your self-limiting patterns of thought and behavior and embrace a future filled with purpose and fulfillment.

As you conquer your goals and live your best life, you'll experience a profound sense of joy.

Feeling stuck in a rut can show up in different ways for each of us.

Here are some signs that might help you figure out if you're in a rut:

- You don't feel like your usual self.
- You feel kind of empty inside.
- You don't have the energy or motivation to do things.
- You're not sure where you're headed.
- You're avoiding tasks or barely getting them done.
- You're searching for a reason or purpose.
- Every day seems boring and the same.
- It's like you're just going through the motions, tied down by responsibilities.
- Negative thoughts and feelings are dragging you down.

Striving for a more meaningful and satisfying life requires effort, but it is definitely worth it. It involves introspection - to better understand who you are now and to envision your future clearly. Additionally, it means crafting a detailed plan to bridge the gap and, ultimately, committing to take action.

It's often said that every significant journey begins with a single, small step. So, why not start today? Utilize this book as your guide to turn your aspirations into reality. Consider it a tool to aid you in overcoming obstacles and breaking free from the rut.

CONTENTS

PART IV. STEP 3. ACHIEVE CONSISTENT *PROGRESS*

PART V. NOW WHAT?

LETTER TO THE READER

Many of us go through life without enough intent, foresight, effort, or courage to reach our potential and live the life of our dreams. It is common to tell ourselves that we can't do this, we aren't worthy, and we don't deserve to be successful. We leave ourselves unprepared when an opportunity presents itself.

From time to time, we may get a burst of momentum and start an exercise program or sign up for an evening class to improve a skill that would help us advance at work. But that momentum can fade fast. Getting outside of our comfort zone is, well, uncomfortable, and takes a lot of effort. We easily find justification for talking ourselves out of continuing with the challenge. Instead of working out or studying, we soon return to the road more traveled. That's the road where we lose our focus and give up. It's more comfortable to go out for a beer with friends, or sit on the couch and scroll through social media.

Old, unhelpful habits are hard to break. It's easier to allow distractions or other people, who claim to be our well-meaning advisors, decide what is best for us. But, at some point, your unhappiness, or even anger, with the way your life is going can stop you in your tracks. Perhaps you've recently experienced the sting of losing a job, gone through a heartbreaking breakup, or faced a health scare that turned your world upside down. After one of these events, will you have a moment of clarity and exclaim, "Now's the time to go for it and do something truly meaningful with my life."

I've been through a lot and that's why I poured my heart and soul into researching and writing this book. I found myself stuck in a job that just didn't fit, ended up marrying the wrong person and then went through the gut-wrenching experience of a divorce. And if that wasn't enough, I was later hit with a cancer diagnosis. Talk about a triple whammy, right? In those moments, I felt utterly lost, hopeless, and filled with regret.

Yet, I refused to give up. I firmly believed that life held so much more for me. The burning desire to push beyond my comfort zone consumed me. Thus, I embarked on an enlightening journey of learning by devouring books written by experts on living a purposeful life. For over three years, I've soaked up wisdom from all sorts of places, carefully sifting through the best advice to create a life-changing process that has helped me discover my real purpose and actively live it. This process, which I named Purpose, Plan, and Progress, became my invaluable personal roadmap.

This book represents just one outcome of how my life improved through changing my thoughts and actions while pursuing my dreams. My only regret is not having acquired this knowledge earlier. The purpose of my book is to provide you with everything you need to uncover your purpose and live the life of your dreams. It serves as the ultimate guide, directing you toward a transformative and positive change, much like it did for me.

Are you ready to embark on the road less traveled and bring your dream vision of the future to life? If so, it's time to ignite the fire of change within you. It's time to invest your time and energy into acquiring the knowledge and skills needed to turn that vision into reality. It's time to summon the courage to never give up, even in the face of challenges. No more just existing and playing it safe. It's time to let your friends know you'll catch up with them later and then silence your cell phone. It's time to get ready to embrace the opportunities that will come knocking on your door.

By learning and applying the simple yet powerful 3-Step Process and life skills shared in this book, you'll break free from limitations and shape your own unique path. This journey is lifelong, and the sooner you begin, the more time you'll have to relish the rewards. Before you know it, you'll wake up every morning feeling grateful for the life you're living. So, what does your dream life look like?

No matter how far you've strayed or how many mistakes you've made, remember it's never too late to break free from limiting thoughts and behaviors, make necessary changes, and find your way back to your true path. We all possess the ability to unlock our true potential and live the life we've always dreamed of, and this book is your golden opportunity to turn that potential into reality. Your extraordinary life awaits!

Jay Nesbit

INTRODUCTION

Are you struggling to live a meaningful life? Does your life feel a little off? Maybe you wake up feeling depleted, sad, burned-out, or unfulfilled. Perhaps your days feel aimless, stressful, or like you're just wasting your time. Maybe you battle with a nagging disappointment that you were meant to do more.

These negative thoughts and feelings could result from your trying to fulfill someone else's expectations, maybe from friends or family telling you what to do with your life. Perhaps it comes from not living up to your own vision or expectations for your life. Possibly you have incorrect beliefs about yourself and the world around you that are holding you back. Maybe your job doesn't mean anything more than the paycheck, and you don't feel noticed or appreciated.

Another reason for feeling stuck arises when you're just going through the motions of life, without having specific goals or clarity about what you should pursue. The idea of change, and the prospect of taking full responsibility for its outcomes, might seem daunting. Nevertheless, it's something we all need to do if we want to be in the driver's seat of our own lives.

If you're not in that seat yet, I strongly believe I can get you there and improve how you feel about your life. It's going to be your job to show up with a strong desire and commitment to invest your time and energy. But, if you're ready and can make this commitment, learning and following the 3-Step Process in this book will seriously change your life. You're free to move forward at your own speed, but before long, you'll begin to make strides toward living a more purposeful life. Of course, there can always be unpredictable events beyond anyone's control, so progress can be delayed, and there are no guarantees of outcome.

When your life doesn't feel right, you need to find the courage and determination to overcome inertia and fear. You need to discover what it is you want, understand what is holding you back, and identify what you need to do differently to find fulfillment in life. Understand that what got you here is not going to get you there. You'll need to adopt a new mindset, attitude, and behavior. Looking for shortcuts or quick fixes is not going to get you where you want to go in the long run. Working on a life-changing process takes time and effort.

Get ready for a remarkable transformation as your vision for the future becomes an empowering roadmap, bridging the divide between where you stand today and the destination of your dreams. As you work through the 3-Step Process, you'll gather invaluable insights to improve your habits and acquire essential skills, enabling you to craft a clear plan with specific, attainable goals. With each step forward on your authentic path, a newfound sense of confidence, accomplishment and fulfillment will envelop you. Equipped with tools to overcome obstacles, you'll gradually build momentum, propelling yourself toward the life you've always desired.

Before embarking on a journey to somewhere you have never been before, it's wise to seek guidance from those who have triumphed on similar paths, equipping you with essential resources and forewarning you of potential challenges. Drawing upon the collective wisdom of numerous experts, I included the best of their advice to shape this 3-Step Process. As you move forward, you may encounter navigational hazards, but fear not, for you will be fully equipped to skillfully navigate around them.

The process is set up to assist you in making big changes to a life that may feel empty. It will help you reveal your real *purpose*, make a *plan* to be your best self, and consistently make *progress*, even when things get tough.

Don't rely on procrastination or luck to lead you to a meaningful life. Neither of these is a winning strategy. Instead, it's time to adopt a new approach. Prepare yourself, put in effort, and stay strong to reach your desired destination. As you dedicate yourself to this demanding yet highly rewarding journey, you'll wake up each morning with a passionate fire and eagerness for the adventures that await.

I think that anyone, no matter their age, can make better choices that really matter in their life. By using the 3-Step Process, a teenager can explore different options for what to do after graduating high school. It can guide a person in mid-career who feels lost at work or in their personal life. And it can benefit someone nearing retirement, wondering what's next in life.

Each one of us has the capacity to overcome hardships and obstacles. We have the choice, at every moment, to take responsibility and be accountable for what we do with our lives. If you're eager to take the wheel and embrace fresh opportunities, here's what each section will empower you to learn:

Part I presents the 3-Step Process that will guide you forward. Part II explains how to use self-reflection to uncover your natural aptitudes, passions, and values, and then use this knowledge to reveal your purpose.

Part III describes how to set goals and make plans to close the gap between where you are now and where you want to be. Part IV helps you understand why you need to commit to taking action every day. You'll also discover the skills to learn, the habits to improve, and effective ways to remain resilient and navigate the challenges you will encounter on your journey of progress.

Lastly, in Part V, we will examine the application of the three steps—*Purpose, Plan, and Progress*—in midlife careers.

Starting something new can be hard, and maintaining it can

be even tougher. However, it all begins if you simply focus on taking that one small step today.

One final point. When you reach the end of each chapter, you will see this stop sign image preceding *Journal prompts* and *Recommended sources for learning more about each topic.* By dedicating time and effort to engage with these activities, you'll begin to make gradual, consistent progress and shift the way you think, feel, and act. Ready? If your answer is yes, let's begin.

PART I

THE 3-STEP PROCESS

1. WHAT IS THE 3-STEP PROCESS?

*The two most important days in life are
the day you were born and the day you find out why.*
— MARK TWAIN

Do you hope to enjoy your life or just endure it?
— KEN ROBINSON

Rut – a habit or pattern of behavior that has become dull and unproductive but is hard to change.

Authentic life – living your life according to your own values, aptitudes, and passions regardless of the pressure that you are under to do otherwise.

Meaningful life – living a life with purpose, significance, fulfillment, and satisfaction.

This book is your key to unlocking a world of endless possibilities and embracing the unique person you were truly meant to be. You are about to discover a powerful process that leads to a life overflowing with purpose and deep meaning. Prepare to find the life-changing answers to three important questions that we've all wondered about at some point:

- *"How did I end up where I am today?"*
- *"Is there more to life than what I'm experiencing right now?"*
- *"Who am I really, at my core?"*

The 3-Step Process of Purpose, Plan, and Progress is designed to be easily understandable and applicable to vital areas of your life, including career, self-care, financial independence, relationships, lifestyle choices, and more. However, I won't sugarcoat it; it does require effort on your part. By diligently following this process, you'll bridge the gap between your current situation and your desired destination. Get ready to unlock a renewed sense of joy and purpose in your life. Here's a glimpse into what you can expect from each step:

Step 1. Uncover your unique *purpose* through self-reflection that reveals your true or authentic self. You will ask yourself questions like "Why do I think, feel and act the way I do?" "What do I like to do?" "What am I good at?" "What do I value in life?" Two helpful routes for effective reflection are acting mindful and journaling. Effective introspection allows you to better understand your current situation.

Completing Step 1 leads to you becoming fully aware of your purpose, also known as your "why." Your purpose is your central, motivating aim in life. It drives and energizes you and provides you with a sense of direction for everything you do. Knowing your purpose simplifies decision-making and goal setting.

Step 2. Now that you have self-understanding, have identified your purpose, and know your starting point, you can visualize where you want to go and develop a *plan* to get there. You'll learn to choose large and small goals and action steps that all correspond with your purpose. Your plan will include making the best use of your time and energy.

You'll know if you have chosen the right goals because you will feel enjoyment as you pursue those goals in Step 3. Your days will feel interesting and meaningful. It will feel like what you are doing is what you were born to do.

Step 3. The final step is to show up and make progress. To make successful progress as you take action on your plan, you will want to acquire a toolkit full of knowledge, skills and good habits. These essential personal qualities enable you to persist even in the face of mistakes and obstacles that arise on your chosen path. You'll learn to control unhelpful thoughts and emotions.

When it comes to accomplishing what truly matters to you, there are no magical shortcuts or quick fixes. None of us are born with the knowledge of how to live life to the absolute fullest. It calls for an unwavering desire to initiate the journey, a steadfast commitment to continuous learning and evolution, and the remarkable courage to conquer fear and embrace risks.

But let me assure you, the reward is immeasurable: it's about unleashing a life that surpasses even your wildest dreams, filling each moment with authentic fulfillment and limitless joy. That's what it means to be true to yourself and live your best life.

I am genuinely excited to work with you on achieving your vision. However, it's important to acknowledge, once again, that reaching your full potential requires effort and dedication on your part. Together, we will embark on a life-changing journey that will shape the rewarding life you were meant to live.

In a nutshell: Picture the life you want, and know what you want to change. Start from where you are, using what you have. Make a plan and take action. Be patient and learn from any bumps along the way. Take good care of yourself and keep going strong.

JOURNAL PROMPTS

Spend 15–30 minutes to reflect on the following prompts and journal your thoughts:

- If you could relive an experience in your life, what would it be, and would you change anything about it?
- What are five things that make you happy?
- Describe your decision-making process. Can you improve it?
- What have you learned from your past decisions?
- Write about three of your big life goals.

RECOMMENDED RESOURCES TO LEARN MORE ON THIS TOPIC

Book: *What Now?* by Ann Patchett

Podcast: *Life Without Limits* by Nic Vujicic

2. HOW DID I END UP HERE?

One of the greatest regrets in life is being what others would want you to be, rather than being yourself.
— SHANNON L. ALDER

Be defined by your vision of the future and not your memory of the past.
— DR. JOE DISPENZA

Feeling stuck – when you spend half your day figuring out which task you should take on first and the other half ruminating over the fact that you wasted so much time deciding.

Hurry sickness –a mixture of anxiety and restlessness that is often accompanied by a continual feeling of urgency.

Life moves fast. Are you on the path to where you want to go? Do you know your purpose, set appropriate goals, and make daily progress toward them? If not, are you ready to change what you are doing and become fulfilled and purposeful? Remember, the approaches that led you to feeling stuck won't be the ones to get you unstuck. As you start to make changes, don't try to do too much too fast. You'll find that small steps, if taken consistently, will turn into large gains.

From my analysis, I've identified eight common reasons why people might feel stuck in life:

1. They are waiting for someone else to solve their problems or make decisions for them.
2. They give up too easily when things get tough.
3. They keep doing the same thing over and over again and expecting different results.
4. They don't believe their life can get better.
5. They are holding on to past experiences or regrets.
6. They are not taking care of themselves or investing in their growth and development.
7. They are hanging out with other people who also feel stuck or negative.
8. They are terrified of making mistakes or taking risks.

Perhaps, as you sip your morning coffee, you find yourself contemplating the twists and turns that led you to this moment. How did you end up here, in this house, this job, this life? The years seemed to have slipped by so quickly, leaving you with a yearning for a deeper understanding of the choices that shaped your path.

In my late thirties, I felt stuck in my life:

- I was working in a career that I was not passionate about,
- My marriage was headed toward divorce,
- I was not taking good care of myself – working too hard, eating poorly, and not exercising.

I felt exhausted and hopeless. Instead of living with purpose, I was flying by the seat of my pants. Besides not knowing my purpose, I did not have a solid awareness of my abilities, passions, and values. I did not have clear goals or plans. I had an incomplete map of where I was and where I wanted to go. I was certainly not living up to my potential.

Once my marriage crashed and burned and I was eager to escape my rut and redefine my path ahead, I made the decision to embrace change. I decided it was time for me to pursue a life that felt more meaningful. For the next several years, I read books, listened to podcasts, and watched videos on what researchers, psychologists, psychiatrists, therapists, and assorted other gurus had to say about how to live a life filled with purpose and meaning.

The idea I heard a lot was that, to rise out of the rut, I needed to become defined by my vision of the future and not by memories of the past. To make that mindset change I had to change my thoughts, which I have heard defined as the language of the brain. In this book, I share the best of what I learned from the dozens of sources I reviewed. My extensive notes provided me with a clear roadmap for myself. The goal of this book was to share this map, which serves as a guide for others to break free from their own rut.

Uncovering my purpose and developing a vision for my future led me on a journey to living my dream. I learned how to set smarter goals and determine the most effective actions to take toward achieving them. I now wake up excited to get started on another meaningful day. I love what I am doing with my life. My new marriage partner and I share some dreams and remain committed to our vows. And I used the 3-Step Process to slowly reduce my pharmacy hours and use the extra time to write—this book is one of the outcomes. The changes I have made are all in line with my future vison and what I value.

All of us will experience negative events in our lives that can make us realize we are living life without intention, or by the seat of our pants. Once you decide you want to change, there will be ups and downs, failures, and obstacles to overcome, but you'll learn to become resilient. If I could accomplish this, then you can too. And I can help you get started promptly by sharing everything I've learned that has proven effective for me.

The 3-Step Process has been field-tested. Throughout the last few years, I have collaborated with friends, co-workers, and clients from my behavioral health pharmacy practice. They all shared a common sentiment – feeling trapped and unable to envision a way forward for themselves. When a few of them opted to apply the process, it gradually resulted in more meaningful and fulfilling changes in their lives as well. I'm confident it will work for you too, provided you're driven to change and determined not to give up. It will alter the way you see yourself and the world around you.

If you find that any of the eight common reasons for feeling stuck resonate with you, it's time to take that crucial first step—and that is to accept your situation for what it is. From there, embrace the willingness to venture beyond your comfort zone, knowing that the outcome may be unpredictable. Taking the first step is hard, but implementing change in your life requires just as much dedication. You'll need a positive attitude, a burning desire, steadfast courage, and a willingness to put in the necessary effort. This book is your map; read it and apply its guidance to steer you along your journey.

Convince yourself that you no longer want to tolerate the feeling of living a life that falls short of your potential. Allow yourself to feel frustration and decide to make a change. Avoid getting distracted by activities that lack meaning. You will need to move out of your comfort zone, which will make you feel vulnerable, but that's what it takes to learn and grow. Many people choose to play it safe their entire lives. And that's how they end up here. But you don't need to stay here.

Before I end this chapter I want to mention the benefits of acting mindful and keeping a journal. To gather your thoughts and gain a deeper understanding of your feelings, practicing mindfulness is the key. This approach enables you to identify their origins, acknowledge them without judgment, and take proactive stops to take care of yourself rather than to continue dwelling in self-pity.

To boost the effectiveness of mindfulness, commit to documenting your thoughts in a journal. By capturing them in writing and revisiting them later, you'll reinforce your focus and stay on course. Thoughts and ideas have a tendency to fade away if not promptly recorded, so seize the opportunity to preserve them for your continued growth and clarity. We will discuss both of these powerful actions, in more detail, in the next chapter.

In a nutshell: I have heard Tony Robbins state that we all need a compelling future to move toward. If you experience fear, worry, complacency, anxiety, insecurity, self-doubt, self-loathing, or hurry sickness, it's crucial to transform your thoughts into ones that are more positive and supportive. Your current pattern of thinking, feeling, and reacting is what brought you here. To change your life, you must change this pattern. Just working harder won't get you unstuck. Thinking about change can be scary, but it's an opportunity for you to experience freedom, growth, and improvement.

Excited to move on to Step 1? Fantastic! We'll begin by examining how practicing mindfulness can help us gain a deeper understanding of ourselves and guide us toward uncovering our purpose.

JOURNAL PROMPTS

- Are you a city, country, or beach person?
- If it were easy, what would you change today about yourself and with your life?
- Are you an introvert or an extrovert? How has it shaped your life?
- Describe your dream life.

RECOMMENDED RESOURCES
TO LEARN MORE ON THIS TOPIC

Book: *Who Am I?* by Siri Ramana Maharshi

Video: *The Strangest Secret in the World* by Earl Nightingale

PART II

STEP 1

Uncover Your Unique *Purpose*

3. MINDFULNESS

Introspection and reflection act as
powerful catalysts in personal growth.
— GAUR GOPAL DAS

Your visions will become clear only
when you can look into your own heart.
Who looks outside, dreams; who looks inside, awakens.
— C.G. JUNG

Mindfulness – focusing awareness on the present moment.

Flow – a state where you are completely absorbed and engrossed in an activity.

Adopting an organized approach to thinking is among the most valuable life skills. Thinking is the way we talk to ourselves, often referred to as self-talk. As most of us are aware, our thoughts can travel in many different directions. Our diverse range of ideas and opinions lead to us experiencing a wide range of emotions, from negative to positive. Practicing mindfulness teaches you to pay attention to your thoughts, analyze their source, and then change them if they are keeping you stuck.

We can act thoughtlessly if we are in a hurry, anxious, or bored. Like when we press an elevator button multiple times to make it get to our floor faster. Or when we check our phones for messages or emails one minute after the last time we checked. Or we reach for a snack when we are not really hungry. Or we find ourselves getting angry with someone because we think they are moving too slowly. These mindless activities are the result of unmanaged thoughts.

If you experience this type of mindless behavior, it's time to start managing your thoughts. To do this, pay attention to your thoughts, feelings, and behaviors as they occur. When you experience a negative or harmful emotion like fear or anxiety, stop and immediately identify the feeling, and write it down. Then ask yourself:

1. What were you thinking or saying to yourself that led to the feeling?
2. Name the negative feeling. Is it anger, apprehension, frustration, fear, shame, grief?
3. How did the feeling lead you to act or react?

Mindfulness encourages us to cultivate a sense of calmness, gratitude, and compassion in our thoughts and actions. The following outlines a process designed to assist you in slowing down and actively managing your thinking:

1. Where and what to bring. Gather a pen and a journal, and mute your cell phone. Seek out a comfortable, quiet, and secluded space where you can think without interruption. Many individuals find meditation sessions beneficial. For meditation suggestions, explore websites such as headspace.com or tenpercent.com.

2. Prepare your mind. Begin by relaxing with long, deep breaths. Pay attention to the sounds, sights, and scents around you as you clear your mind, concentrate, and connect with your sense of enthusiasm and hopefulness.

3. Ask yourself questions. First, pose gratitude questions like "What are three things I am grateful for today?" or "What is something I did well today?" Your responses can be as straightforward as "I feel healthy today" or "The weather is perfect today." Jot them down.

Next, move on to more contemplative questions, like "What am I feeling right now?" or "What has been occupying my thoughts today?" Through this introspection, you'll develop a more profound self-awareness, prioritizing self-compassion over self-judgment, and searching for solutions to move ahead.

Ask *what* questions, not *why* ones, to find answers that are objective, positive, and empower you to act on your insights. "What surprised or frustrated you?" "What are the steps I need to take in the future to do a better job?" "What have I learned from my mistakes?"

When your mind wanders, make note of any important random thoughts and then get back to focusing on the question you are trying to answer. Keep the session positive. Go easy on yourself if you struggle with the process. Pause for a moment and focus again on your breathing to help you relax and refocus.

Certain questions may demand more thought and contemplation than others. In such cases, feel free to revisit the same question over several days or weeks. For instance, "What type of work would excite and fulfill me more than what I am doing now?" or "What can I do to improve a relationship?" Allow yourself time to find creative solutions. Drill deeper by repeatedly asking yourself "What else?'

4. Schedule regular sessions. Begin with short sittings, like five minutes twice a week, to get started. Gradually increase the length and number of sessions. To stay accountable, have a friend call and ask about your progress.

For effective journaling, be sure to record your thoughts and feelings during each session. This allows you to revisit and probe deeper into these questions in subsequent mindfulness sessions. You'll observe that as you focus on a topic, your brain continues to generate ideas even after you've moved on to other tasks.

Ideas or solutions frequently come to mind when I'm occupied with familiar, routine tasks that allow my mind to wander, such as eating alone, getting dressed, driving a familiar route or taking a peaceful walk. To ensure I don't lose these valuable insights, I always carry a small notepad and pen with me to jot them down.

Mindfulness isn't a practice that demands a magic ritual. We all naturally have thoughts and feelings. When we dislike them and react poorly to their presence, we often attempt to push them away. The distinction in mindfulness practice lies in intentionally observing and labeling our thoughts and emotions, without passing judgment, reacting negatively, or attempting to suppress or disregard them.

When learning something new, you need the desire to start and the resilience to keep going. Adopt a positive attitude, use your imagination, and let your creativity flow. Keep in mind that acting mindful is a skill that improves with practice, so be patient with yourself. As you get more comfortable you'll find yourself looking forward to each new experience. Choose to make mindfulness a part of your lifestyle, and watch it enrich your journey.

A process I read about, referred to as Mind Sculpture, is a form of mental rehearsal. It uses mindfulness and works like this:[4]

---

4 Ian Robertson, *Mind Sculpture*, 2000.

- Imagine, with all your senses, that you are actually engaged in an action. This could be something you fear, such as giving a presentation in front of a large group or taking a final exam in a tough class.
- What do you see, feel, smell, taste, and hear?
- Routinely imagine yourself successfully doing something, appreciating the positive results while engaging all your senses. Visualize the event vividly in your mind.

Mind Sculpture is a structured and reassuring program designed to develop the skills required for achievement. Through this method, you effectively address and neutralize fear while enhancing your self-confidence, setting the stage for tangible success when you finally execute what you've been preparing for.

It's important to remember that we often create barriers that prevent us from achieving complete self-understanding. These hurdles arise when we block certain thoughts from our minds because they are unpleasant, provoke anxiety, or challenge our existing self-image. Additionally, our brain's limited capacity for total recall, and its accuracy, may impede our ability to access all the information we need.

Some of us may have experienced major trauma in our past and can't seem to push past the recurring pain and discomfort. In these cases, I advise you to seek out the help of a professional therapist who will assist you in taking a deep dive into your thought processes.

Practicing mindfulness brings forth numerous positive benefits, including:

- You learn to replace negative thoughts with positive ones.
- It helps you cope with difficult life events and negative emotions.
- It improves your attention and concentration.

- You stop spending time dwelling on the past or fearing the future and start experiencing moments in the present.
- It stimulates your creativity.
- It enhances your performance in work, sports, or academics.
- It promotes better health by reducing stress, lowering your blood pressure, and boosting your immune system.
- It strengthens your relationships.

Self-reflection and analysis are a great opportunity to change behaviors that bother us. Once you identify the thought–feeling–behavior cycle, you can cultivate the desire to change it. Understand that change is not easy and will take time and effort to transform an unwanted behavior. We will talk about changing harmful habits in a later chapter.

Use mindfulness to slow down and relax when negative thoughts or stress arise. This practice enables you to respond calmly in emotionally charged situations, such as during a relationship disagreement or after receiving a negative review at work. Additionally, you'll gain insights into developing self-love and compassion.

The final mental state I want to discuss regarding mindfulness is known as *flow* or being *in the zone*. It's a state of intense engagement, focus, and contentment that arises when you are absorbed in an activity or task you love doing.

Imagine being so immersed in what you're doing that time and space seem to fade away. You experience a surge of creativity and productivity that drives you to excel at your task. This deep enjoyment of the process brings about a profound sense of happiness and fulfillment in life. This is what a flow state feels like. To achieve this blissful state, focus on one thing at a time and set aside a chunk of time when you can tune out the noise and distractions around you.

Flow states are recognized for their ability to enhance

creativity, boost performance, and spark innovation. These experiences are considered profound enough to contribute to an individual's overall life satisfaction.

In a nutshell: Self-reflection through mindfulness is a skill that gradually improves as you make every effort to become more proficient. This skill will be invaluable to you throughout the entire 3-Step Process. To be effective, it's crucial to relax, as stress can make it difficult to focus. By gaining a deeper understanding of yourself, you create a more fulfilling life.

In the upcoming chapter, we'll explore the power of journaling and how it can enhance your ability to remember important details, leading to a greater sense of wellbeing.

JOURNAL PROMPTS

- What are three things you are grateful for today?
- What things do you look forward to in the day to come?
- What's making you feel anxious or stressed right now?
- Are you feeling satisfied? If not, what are your biggest obstacles to experiencing contentment?
- What activities in your life bring you joy, and how can you incorporate them more frequently?

RECOMMENDED RESOURCES TO LEARN MORE ON THIS TOPIC

Book: *Mindfulness Activities for Adults* by Matthew Rezac

Podcast: *10% Happier* with Dan Harris

Podcast: *Mindfulness Mode* with Bruce Langford

4. JOURNALING

I can shake off everything as I write;
my sorrows disappear, my courage is reborn.
— ANNE FRANK

Write what disturbs you, what you fear,
what you have not been willing to speak about.
Be willing to be split open.
— NATALIE GOLDBERG

Journaling – a written record of your thoughts & feelings. Mindfulness in motion.

To fully harness the benefits of this book, it's essential to put what you learn into practice. In addition to mindfulness, a powerful tool for self-understanding, I recommend including journaling as a complementary process. The act of journaling helps you explore your innermost fears, thoughts, and feelings, giving you a chance to know yourself better.

Journaling involves writing down your thoughts, feelings, ambitions, hopes, dreams, and fears. There are no firm rules, although most sources suggest making journaling a routine exercise. You can also sketch or jot down favorite quotations, poems, and to-do lists. You can include photos or pictures too.

As you pour your heart onto paper, you will find solace, clarity, and a sense of release. With each entry, you'll notice your thoughts becoming more organized, your emotions more manageable, and your understanding of yourself deepening. Over time, you will discover that journaling is not only a creative outlet but also a tool for self-reflection and personal growth. It can bring a sense of peace and purpose to your days.

The International Association of Journal Writing (The IAJW) lists eight ideas on what to write in a journal. Consider writing about:

- Your daily activities.
- The things you love and that bring you joy.
- Your goals and actionable steps.
- Your five-year plan.
- Your worries and fears.
- Solutions to your problems.
- Affirmations or positive statements that encourage you.
- What you are grateful for.

To begin, all you need is a pen or pencil and a topic that sparks your interest. Personally, I find a journal that's about 5x8 inches is small enough to carry around yet large enough for comfortable writing. However, the look and feel of a journal are entirely up to your personal taste. You can explore expressive workbooks available at museums and boutiques, or even try special writing instruments designed for journaling. Whatever your preference, take that first step today and start jotting down your thoughts and experiences.

Being mindful and journaling are valuable practices for understanding your daily life and discovering your uniqueness. By enhancing self-awareness and documenting your thoughts, you gain clearer insights into your challenges. You can identify personal triggers for negative thoughts, feelings, and behaviors, leading you to find creative solutions. Additionally, these practices prompt you to reflect on your aspirations and consider the path you want to take from here.

Regular journaling strengthens immune cells. Therefore, if you struggle with stress, depression, or anxiety—all of which lower your ability to fight off disease—keeping a journal can help you gain control of your emotions and mental health, while also improving your physical well-being.[5]

The journal is for your personal use, so feel free to write or include anything you like. To turn journaling into a habit, we follow the same process as forming any habit: by doing it consistently. The following techniques will guide you in establishing a writing routine:

- Start with small steps. Setting a timer for 1–5 minutes to begin feels less intimidating. As you get more comfortable with the process, you can gradually increase the time.
- Any form of taking and saving notes works well. We mentioned pen and paper, but it could also be a program or document on your computer or a note-taking app on your phone. You decide where to start , and you can always try something different later.
- Before starting, try to have an idea about the topic you want to write about. This way, you can quickly focus and make the most of your journaling time, for the best results.
- Try to establish a consistent time for writing each day. Many people find it helpful to journal with their morning coffee, evening tea, after dinner, or whenever

5 James Pennebaker, *Opening Up by Writing It Down*, 2016.

they can be alone with their thoughts and reflections.
- There are no limitations to the topics you can explore in your journal.

Allow your thoughts and feelings to flow freely as you write. For further guidance on journaling, consider attending workshops that teach methods for tuning into your inner truth and gaining a comprehensive self-understanding. Take a look at sites like journaltherapy.com and jounalingworkshops.com to learn more about the workshops they offer. As you improve your journaling skills, this kind of assistance can guide you to push past mental barriers and become more like the person you want to be.

Prompts are a helpful way to begin writing when you're unsure what to write about today. At the end of each chapter, I include some journal prompts to start you thinking and help you probe further into the topics discussed. Additionally, you can explore memories of your school years, write about something you love or fear doing and why, or express what you value most in relationships. The internet offers a wealth of great prompts to get you thinking and writing. As a personal example, I recently received a deck of prompt cards as a creative birthday present.

Effective journal prompts consist of open-ended questions that lead toward deeper self-understanding. To truly benefit, take your time drilling down into your memories. As I mentioned in the previous chapter on mindfulness, you can further consider solutions by journaling about the same question over several days. If I come up with something I want to add to my journal but don't have it with me, I capture the thought on my phone by either texting myself or using a notes app.

A helpful way to stay on track and continue practicing these skills is to share your thoughts or your written work with a supportive network of friends or family members. These are people I trust to have my best interest in mind. They remind me of the reasons behind past decisions or they provide their perspective on events. We go into greater detail on accountability and support networks in Chapter 30.

In a nutshell: Journaling is a powerful method that helps you reflect on your life and take charge of your story. Take it slow and get creative, even if you write just a few lines each time. Journaling reveals patterns in your thoughts and behaviors, showing you what's holding you back or causing stress, and guides you toward discovering your unique purpose, the very essence of *Step 1*.

In the next chapter we'll look at how mindfulness and journaling contribute to a deeper self-understanding. Developing this self-awareness brings you closer to unveiling your purpose and enhancing your life.

JOURNAL PROMPTS

- Do you feel happy with your life right now?
- What did you make progress on that made today better than yesterday?
- What can you make progress on tomorrow that will make tomorrow better than today?
- Who or what do you aspire to be?

RECOMMENDED RESOURCES TO LEARN MORE ON THIS TOPIC

Book: *The Great Book of Journaling* by Eric Maisel and Lynda Monk

Video: *How to Journal* by JetPens

5. SELF-UNDERSTANDING

*Not until we are lost do we begin
to understand ourselves.*
— HENRY DAVID THOREAU

*Knowing yourself is
the beginning of all wisdom.*
— ARISTOTLE

Self-understanding – the ability of the individual to understand his or her own thoughts, feelings, behaviors, motives, actions, and reactions.

Self-reflection – to observe and analyze yourself in order to learn and grow as a person.

Living inauthentically – trying to be someone you are not. You disregard your own wants, needs, thoughts, and feelings in place of the wants and needs of others.

Self-understanding is essential for living a genuine and purposeful life. It paves the way for personal and professional growth.

When you truly know yourself, making decisions that align with your purpose becomes more natural, and you can avoid choices that lead to distress. With self-awareness, you can choose compatible friends, partners, a meaningful career, and a place to live that aligns with your true passions, and values.

We gain self-awareness through introspection, which involves reflecting on our thoughts, emotions, and memories to understand their meaning. Feedback from others also helps us see ourselves objectively and identify areas for improvement. Self-understanding should guide you in setting appropriate goals and plans, which is *Step 2* of the process. When there's a mismatch, you might feel discomfort or a sense that something is off. On the other hand, a lack of self-understanding can lead us to act in ways that don't truly reflect our inner desires, causing us to live inauthentically.

For much of my life, I accepted a culture that emphasized pursuing success and happiness through external achievements and material possessions. Even with impressive accomplishments and possessions, a sense of emptiness persisted, prompting me to begin a journey of self-understanding.

My aim was to gain clarity about what truly mattered to me and what I genuinely desired from life. As I probed deeper, I discovered that authentic fulfillment and lasting happiness arise from aligning my actions and choices with my deepest aspirations and core values, rather than seeking superficial markers of success defined by others' expectations.

Do you ever feel hopeless, confused, or angry about the way your life is going? Many of us go blindly through life, not thinking about who we are, what we are doing, or where we are going. We can feel befuddled about our actions, or inactions, that go against what we think we want for our lives. Why did I do that?

Inner tension arises when you find yourself doing something differently than you wish to, causing a misalignment between your thoughts and actions with your goals or purpose. Examples of tension include:

- Eating a couple of donuts when your goal is to lose fifteen pounds.
- Not having taken the time to exercise for several months, even though you promised yourself you would work out a few times each week to increase your strength, balance, and energy.
- Continuing to work at the same unsatisfying job despite telling yourself for years that you want to explore better career options.
- Procrastinating due to anxiety and fear in a difficult situation when you want to feel and act more confidently under stress.

You need to deal with this tension if you want to change and be successful with your personal and professional development. To do this successfully, you need to learn more about yourself. Self-reflection is an effective way to change your life and make you more successful.

Most of us are familiar with the Greek adage "know thyself." Socrates interpreted this to mean that you must know yourself before you can claim to know anything else. It is foundational to our growth. If purpose is our 'why', then self-understanding is our 'how'. It's a map that helps us navigate our inner landscape. It involves gaining insight into our thoughts, feelings, and actions. How well do you really know yourself today?

While most people *believe* they are self-aware, only 10%–15% of people actually are. One reason is that we all are super busy and distracted, making it difficult to find time to focus our mind and effectively self-reflect.[6]

---

6 Tasha Eurich, *Insight*, 2018.

One more obstacle we encounter is the way we perceive ourselves and the world, shaped by the filters we have installed within us. These filters are a blend of ideas, emotions, values, and past experiences, combined with our individual personalities. The view we have through these filters gives rise to stories about our identity and how we perceive ourselves to be.

Part of self-understanding is to realize that many of the stories we tell ourselves are not true. Filters can distort reality. For instance, if you ask yourself the question "What am I like?" you might answer with self-limiting thoughts like "I'm not good enough," or "I always mess things up." These answers are part of the stories we tell ourselves and are not based on fact. Perhaps you heard this a lot when you were growing up. These become the made-up realities that we have constructed for ourselves and come to believe. We learn to believe things we hear repetitively, even if they aren't true.

Use this realization to discover your truth from introspection, and not some preconceived notion of who you thought you were. Once you know the truth, it can be used to sync your outer life (the way you act) with your inner life (the way you think and feel). It will help you learn the source of what you believe, which can make you more resolute to learn more about what makes you tick.

Through my reading, I have discovered that when we convince ourselves that we had a terrific childhood and later take the time to deeply reflect on our past, we may uncover buried traumatic experiences. This newfound awareness that our early years were not as ideal as we believed can be disheartening and disillusioning.[7]

It's completely alright to uncover the truth about your past and recognize the root causes of your distress. However, it's important to remember that dwelling solely on self-reflection

---

7 Gabor Mate, *The Myth of Normal*, 2022.

can prevent you from moving forward. Once you've gained this newfound self-awareness, you possess the power to take proactive steps toward self-improvement and get what you really want out of your precious life.

Do that by refocusing your energy and efforts on shaping a brighter future that aligns with your authentic self. Remember, it's not just about understanding your story, but using that understanding as a catalyst for positive change and personal growth.

Many of us respond to negative emotions, caused by unmanaged distress or trauma in our lives, by using drugs or alcohol as an attempt to bury our feelings and not have to deal with them. Managed introspection of our negative feelings can help us understand and deal with them and avoid the impulse to engage in self-harm.

Self-reflection is an important skill to learn and continually develop. It helps you process thoughts and feelings, unraveling the reasons behind them. It offers you a look back at all that you have accomplished and also what you need to still work on and improve. It allows you to assess if you are truly happy and content with your life and, if unsatisfied, explore potential avenues for change. It guides you in setting and attaining your goals.

Self-knowledge provides these benefits:

- Enhanced ability to identify and comprehend our emotions.
- Improved interpersonal relationships.
- Heightened life satisfaction.
- Increased well-being, self-esteem, and confidence.
- Reduced stress levels.
- Enhanced skills in emotional regulation.
- Augmented capacity to refine habits.
- Elevated academic and creative accomplishments.
- Enhanced decision-making and choices in your daily life.

If you are willing to invest the time, effort, and struggle to confront your misconceptions, achieving a comprehensive and accurate understanding of your true self marks the starting point of a more rewarding life journey. Embrace the authentic core of who you are. Self-understanding serves as the initial step to bridging the gap between your current position and your desired destination.

In a nutshell: Self-reflection is an ongoing journey of discovering your true self and using that knowledge to shape a fulfilling future. It guides you to make decisions aligned with your authentic self and leads to increased empathy, positivity, growth, and happiness. Through self-reflection, you don't become a different person, but you evolve into a better version of yourself.

I know it can feel overwhelming to examine your life. Memories can be powerful. Remember, it's about learning not judging. Your past doesn't have to dictate your future, and seeking support from a therapist can be beneficial if you are facing challenges. It's essential to master this step before proceeding further. The more authentic you behave, the more you will like yourself—and so will others.

A significant aspect of living authentically is understanding your personality. This self-awareness allows you to compare your traits with others and predict your reactions in various situations. In the next chapter, we'll explore the topic of personality and its potential for change.

JOURNAL PROMPTS

- How would you describe yourself as a kid and teenager?
- What five pieces of advice would you have given yourself at age 14, if you could go back in time?
- Describe one or two significant life events that helped shape you into who you are today.
- What difficult thoughts or emotions come up most frequently for you?
- How does work fulfill you? Does it leave you wanting more?

RECOMMENDED RESOURCES TO LEARN MORE ON THIS TOPIC

Book: *Trick Mirror: Reflections on Self-Delusion* by Jia Tolentino

Book: *Start Where You Are: A Journal for Self-Exploration* by Meera Lee Patel

Video: *Increase Your Self-Awareness with One Simple Fix* by Tasha Eurich

Video: *Introspection: Looking Within* by Colin Gagne

6. PERSONALITY

*The most important kind of freedom
is to be what you really are.*
— JIM MORRISON

*I hold that a strongly marked personality
can influence descendants for generations.*
— BEATRIX POTTER

Personality – the characteristic patterns of thoughts,
feelings, and behaviors that make a person unique.

The development of personality hinges on self-understanding,
as it provides individuals with insights into their true selves.
It's still up for debate how much of personality comes from the
genes you're born with and how much is learned after birth.
Averaging out the prevailing views in the research, it'd be about
40% coming from genes, and the rest learned or acquired from
life experiences and trends in your culture.[8]

Understanding your own personality and being aware of

---

8 Steven Pinker, *The Blank Slate*, 2003.

who you truly are can help make sense of your unique ways of thinking, feeling, and behaving, even if it's not exactly clear about the nature vs. nurture percentages. It also sheds light on how you might act in different situations. Moreover, this self-awareness allows you to think about and improve the parts of yourself that you have learned and developed over time. While we can't change what happens in our lives, we do have control over how we respond to those events. This control is part of living a fulfilling life.

We all create our own personality in important ways. During your early years you choose and add little character traits, mannerisms, ways of talking and walking, facial expressions, and gestures. Even ways of thinking and believing are borrowed, imitated, and made your own. You've taken these little bits and blended them into – you![9]

The 60% of learned personality elements that you acquired when you were growing up might not align with who you desire to be as an adult. Therefore, it's a good idea to occasionally step back and examine what you have created, assessing whether you want to remodel or reshape it. Ask yourself if these elements truly reflect your updated vision for yourself?

While certain traits like coloring, bone structure, and height are inherited, much of who you are is a result of your choices. You have the right, and perhaps even the obligation, to remake yourself exactly as you see fit. Embracing personality development as a lifelong goal can lead to personal growth and fulfillment.

Personality tests are useful for learning more about yourself. You can take one of these tests and read about the common personality types on websites like personalityperfect.com or truity.com. Your type, and its accompanying descriptive traits, can help you understand who you are and why you act the way you do. However, some of described traits for your characteristic

---

9 Mildred Newman and Bernard Berkowitz, *How to Take Charge of Your Life*, 1977.

type might sound nothing like you.

I took the quiz on 16personalities.com. They pegged me as a 'Logistician' personality type. Those of us with this type of personality are likely to:

- spend an entire weekend by themselves without feeling bored;
- enjoy having a general plan for each day;
- avoid risky or unpredictable situations;
- prefer realistic art to abstract art;
- find it difficult to relate to people who let their emotions guide them;
- dislike team projects.

But Logisticians, like me, struggle in areas like finding, or keeping, a partner; learning to relax and improvise; or reaching the upper rungs of a career ladder.

I think these websites and their personality types can help you with your self-analysis, but don't lean on them too heavily. As previously mentioned, we tend to believe inaccurate things about ourselves that were instilled by others. If we use these false beliefs about ourselves in answering some of the test questions, we may get misleading results. Plus, many of us are a combination of two or more personality types. I suggest taking a few different personality tests and then looking for character traits that are repetitive.

Ask yourself which characteristics sound right to you and start developing your own personality profile. Through mindful self-reflection, continue seeking answers to questions about who you are, how you should live, and where you belong.

Many modern psychologists suggest that overall personality is relatively fixed and stable throughout life. However, one psychologist explains that his findings shatter the false belief that we are permanently locked into negative personality traits – traits that can hinder our potential for happiness and success. Once you gain a better understanding of who you are now, how others perceive you, and which aspects of yourself you'd like to change, it's possible to adjust your personality and improve yourself.[10]

The constant interaction between genetics and the environment can help shape how personality is expressed. For example, you might be genetically predisposed to being friendly and laid back, but working in a high-stress environment could lead you to be more short-tempered and uptight than you would be working in less anxiety-provoking setting.

So, take a good look at your present self. Your sense of self has certainly changed since you initially began shaping your identity. You know a lot more about what works and what doesn't work for you. If you are holding onto a personality trait you don't like, there is a good chance you can change it. However, it requires adapting a positive or growth mindset. If you believe you cannot change, then you will not change.

Besides having a growth mindset and believing you can change, I suggest adding positive, yet realistic, self-affirmations to build your positive self-image and take charge of your life. Say to yourself things like "I am working hard to become a helpful person" or "I am proud how I am learning to stay calm in a stressful environment," even if you aren't feeling that way at the moment. You are reinforcing, in your mind, the kind of person you would like to be. Soon you will start to feel and act the way you envision yourself.

It is unlikely that you will be able to permanently change certain aspects of your personality. An introvert is not going to become an extrovert, for example. However, I believe you can choose to act like an extrovert for short periods of time, like at a party or when doing a presentation at work.

---

10 Gary Small, SNAP!, 2018.

In a nutshell: Personality is displayed in our thoughts, feelings, and behavior. Changing elements of your learned personality is not easy but can lead to personal and professional growth. The change process includes setting goals with small steps, which we will discuss in detail as part of Step 2.

Another characteristic that creates your sense of self comes from an increased understanding of your aptitudes or natural abilities. This is the topic for the next chapter.

JOURNAL PROMPTS

- What is one thing in your life you wish you could change? List three specific actions on how you can make that change.
- What personality traits do you like about yourself and why? What traits don't you like and why?

RECOMMENDED RESOURCES TO LEARN MORE ON THIS TOPIC

Book: *Snap!: Change Your Personality in 30 Days* by Gary Small and Gigi Vorgan

Video: *What Is Personality?* by Personality Psychology

7. APTITUDE

*Artists, musicians, scientists— if you have any kind
of visionary aptitude, it's often something you
don't have a choice in. You have to do it.*
— PATTI SMITH

*Ability is what you are capable of doing.
Motivation determines what you do.
Attitude determines how well you do it.*
— LOU HOLTZ

Aptitude – the potential to learn or excel in a particular field. A natural ability or talent.

Ability – a person's current skill level or competency in a specific area.

Potential – latent qualities or abilities that may be developed and lead to future success or usefulness.

It's common for people to downplay the idea that they have talents. However, everyone possesses aptitudes, which are natural talents they are born with. Having aptitude means having the capacity or potential to learn and excel in a specific area. You would learn quickly and have a high potential, but making the most of your innate talent requires having a positive attitude and a strong desire to practice regularly and extensively.

Some talents may be discovered early in life, while others might remain hidden because the opportunity to explore them never arises. Having a skill that comes naturally to you gives you a competitive advantage. Therefore, it is beneficial to identify your talents and leverage them to your advantage. How can you determine your natural abilities?

One way is to explore new things that interest you and see if you demonstrate potential. Each of us possesses unique aptitudes. A few examples are musical or artistic talent, attention to detail, learning a foreign language, math, sports, humor, or compassion. But there are many more. Start a list of skills that sound interesting to you.

For now, this is a list of your potential aptitudes. You can't know if you might be good at something if you have never tried it. You shouldn't limit yourself to only the aptitudes you know about from your experiences. We are not typically exposed to many potential aptitudes in traditional school or in most homes. It's left up to each of us to expand our horizons by trying activities that sound interesting.

You may need to challenge your own beliefs about what you might be good at doing. Perhaps you believe you are bad at math. Is it possible that this perception is influenced by the way it was taught, primarily through lectures and note-taking, without considering the needs of more visual learners? In most schools, little consideration is given to the individual student's unique learning style. Consequently, many children who may have outstanding abilities for a subject tune out the instructor, perform poorly in the class, and everyone assumes they lack aptitude for that subject.

You can have many aptitudes or areas of potential. Reflecting on the subjects you enjoyed the most while studying in school might be helpful. You can also consider what you like to do in your free time, when you have the freedom to pursue any activity. Additionally, consider what others—teachers, friends, family, etc.—have told you that you are good at?

Another way to assess your potential to learn certain skills is by taking an aptitude test, which is frequently used to evaluate academic potential or career suitability. Many employers ask applicants to complete one of these tests to determine if the applicants have the potential required to excel in the job they are applying for. These tests are only designed to evaluate particular skills or careers. For instance, they can't determine if you have artistic or musical abilities.

One example is the Clevry Ability Tests. Clevry offers tests for numerical, verbal, and abstract abilities. Another example is the KSA or Knowledge, Skills, and Abilities assessment. The KSA evaluates your verbal, written, and comprehension skills, all of which significantly impact your ability to perform a specific job effectively.

Potential employers may not share test results with applicants. Therefore, I suggest that you take an aptitude test independently to access your results. A given aptitude can be applied in various careers that you might not have considered. Take the time to explore career options that align with your natural abilities.

One online test you can take to discover your talents is called the Clifton Strengths. Their website suggests that it's more beneficial to enhance what you are already good at rather than focusing on improving your weaknesses. By developing abilities that you already tend to be proficient in, you increase your chances of success. Plus, you'll likely find more enjoyment in work or activities that make use of your natural talents.

Also, a personality test, such as the one available on mypersonality.net, can illuminate some personal traits. For instance, it can indicate whether you are more comfortable working independently or as part of a team. If you prefer working independently, it might be wise to avoid jobs that require you to be a team leader or supervisor.

This test can also assess how well you handle stress from pressure and deadlines. Some folks shut down and cry, while others thrive under such conditions. Certain careers, such as healthcare, journalism, sales, and others, require you to handle a lot of stress. In these fields, you may face daily pressure and multiple deadlines.

I also suggest taking a moment to reflect on your childhood for potential clues about your aptitudes. Create a list of any dream careers you recall considering, driven by the belief that you would excel in them. The specifics of how different they were from your actual path don't matter for this exercise. Even if you decide to remain in your current role, this process could reveal opportunities to leverage these skills more prominently.

Some of your life experiences may have enhanced your skills in certain areas. For instance, if you moved a lot as a child or were encouraged to try many things outside of your comfort zone, it likely helped you become more flexible and taught you to face challenges and changes with confidence. These skills would be beneficial in many careers.

My final suggestion for discovering your aptitudes is through a business process called a SWOT Analysis. You can learn more about this on the website mindtools.com. SWOT is a technique used to identify potential strengths, weaknesses, opportunities, and threats.

Through introspection and taking a KSA assessment, I have discovered that my natural abilities or skills include:

- **Planning** – I've always liked setting goals and making plans, whether it's for future vacations, saving money for real estate investments, or finishing this book.
- **Managing time** – I'm good at using a daily calendar to keep track of my tasks and for getting things done.
- **Staying focused** – This is really important for my job as a pharmacist. I've seen others struggle with this.
- **Learning** – I can quickly learn new things and use them well. I'm improving my writing skills by reading, watching videos, taking classes, and practicing.
- **Listening to feedback** – I have been told that I am good at listening, staying organized, thinking logically, and staying calm when things are tough. I got better at these things by staying positive and through repetition.

Three activities that captured my interest when I was younger were playing cards, bowling, and golf. I never excelled at any of them, so they might not have been inherent aptitudes for me. However, it's important to remember that even if you are not naturally talented in a particular area, it does not mean that you cannot develop yourself and achieve excellence.

In a nutshell: Understanding your aptitude begins with a journey of self-discovery. Through introspection and exploration, you uncover your talents and natural inclinations toward a particular skill or area of interest. Pay attention to activities that bring you joy and a sense of fulfillment. What you like to do is called your passion. Combining a natural talent with a genuine passion for a particular pursuit can accelerate your journey toward fulfilling your potential.

JOURNAL PROMPTS

- What activities come easy to you?
- What were you good at doing when you were younger?
- What are your strengths at work and in life?
- What activities look interesting to you, but you have not yet tried?

RECOMMENDED RESOURCES TO LEARN MORE ON THIS TOPIC

Book: *Your Natural Gifts* by Margaret Broadley

Video: *What Is Aptitude* by Productivity Guy

8. PASSION

If you can't figure out your purpose, figure out your passion.
For your passion will lead you right into your purpose.
— BISHOP T. D. JAKES

You can choose what you do;
you can't choose what you like to do.
— GRETCHEN RUBIN

Passion – An activity you enjoy doing, that brings you joy, contentment, and engagement.

Desire – having the passion and aspiration to improve your life.

Passion is a deep, personal attraction or enthusiasm that can lead to profound enjoyment and fulfillment. When you are engaged in an activity that ignites your passion, you experience the power of positive energy. This experience varies for each of us. Often, we wonder how someone can find joy in their job when we believe we would dislike it immensely.

Now that you are learning to have a better understanding of who you are, it will be easier to find activities that align with your abilities or aptitudes. If you have innate potential, you can quickly improve your skills with practice. But passion is what makes the real difference. Passion is what makes you want to invest the time and effort needed to practice and develop your skill. When you bring passion, you'll find pleasure in the process and enjoy the journey of improvement. Without adequate self-knowledge you may never learn your passion.

You may not yet know what your passion is, but once you uncover it, you can hopefully create a lifestyle that allows you to engage in that work as your everyday career. Those of us that do this get to say, "I can't believe how lucky I am to be doing what I love." Your passion might be uncovered from a sudden inspiration or come to you gradually. The result is the same.

But, for various reasons, not everyone can make a living from what they love to do, at least not in the early stages. Many people find themselves stuck in jobs they don't enjoy or that don't fulfill them. If that's your situation, it's important to find a way to spend part of your day doing something that engages you and connects to your true passion. You never know where it will lead once you get started. An opportunity can open up that you might never have imagined.

Studies have found that when you engage in activities you enjoy, you experience less stress and have a lower resting heart rate. It helps instill some calm throughout your body, not to mention it injects more positive thoughts into your mind and helps to banish negative ones.[11]

This experience is referred to as internal motivation, which stems from the long-term, pure enjoyment you derive from doing something you love. Additionally, you'll also spend less time procrastinating, because when you engage in what you enjoy, it doesn't feel like a chore. And, if you love doing something, you'll want to keep getting better at it.

---

11 Susan Biali M.D., *Life a Life You Love*, 2010.

In contrast, external motivation arises from the expectation of a future reward, something outside yourself. This type of motivation doesn't last for long. Many of us experience this when we change jobs to earn a raise. However, if it turns out to be work you don't enjoy, the extra pay will not keep you motivated for long.

To learn about your passions, practice mindfulness and journaling. Have a conversation with yourself about subjects you enjoyed in school or like to read about. Consider hobbies that captivate your interest or activities that immerse you in a state of flow. Consider any specific tasks at work that you enjoy and would like to learn more about.

Include all activities that boost your energy, uplift your spirits, bring you joy, and fill you with excitement to do them as often as you can. Make these activities your addiction, not drugs, television, or snacking. In addition, seek input from people you trust about what they believe are your natural strengths or talents.

Explore new opportunities by trying new activities that sound interesting to you. Take a class, ask about volunteer opportunities, or take on a part-time job in a field that sounds like something you would enjoy. Additionally, read books and watch videos that offer insights on discovering your passion.

Conversely, you'll want to avoid activities that evoke negative emotions and become sources of anger, irritation, boredom, frustration, struggle, or anxiety for you. It's important to be aware of what these activities are.

Be patient and persevere. It might take some time to discover your passion, and that's perfectly okay. Don't give up if it doesn't happen as fast as you'd like. Write possibilities into your journal for future consideration, as you explore various ideas. And remember, you don't have to limit yourself to having just one passion. It's not uncommon to realize you have multiple interests.

Once you figure out your aptitudes and passions, if you are fortunate, you can find the perfect job aligned with these. If not, you can pursue your passion as a hobby or something to look forward to after work or over the weekend. Ask someone already doing this work what they enjoy about it, how they got started, and how they learned to master their craft.

For most of us, our lives are the result of chance instead of design. Our interests and personalities start us down an interesting path, but circumstances and opportunities might divert us elsewhere. Life is not necessarily linear, and you'll gain valuable insights once you start taking your first steps toward where you think you want to go. It is often said that action leads to clarity.

For instance, just because you choose to get a degree in art history doesn't mean you will spend your life working in that field. You may begin your career there and a few years later receive an unexpected offer from a major business to become the curator and fundraiser for their extensive and growing art collection. This new job can turn out to be an even better fit for your abilities and provide you with greater fulfillment.

To broaden your thinking about potential areas of interest, here is a list of passions that others have discovered:

- Health and wellness – focusing on your physical and mental wellbeing.
- Personal growth – improving your skills, knowledge, habits, or other personal qualities.
- Community service or social engagement – providing care and assistance to people in an underserved neighborhood, advocating for justice, or addressing environmental issues.
- Relationships – building connections and strong bonds with people around you.
- Money management – understanding and improving your financial fitness.

- Education – acquiring new skills and possibly teaching others.
- Creativity – expressing yourself through art or writing.
- Entrepreneurship – starting your own business to solve problems for others.
- Animal rights – adopting or spending time with animals in need of attention.
- Technology – learning and sharing the benefits of computer programs or phone apps.

I have read that truly living means doing things not out of obligation, expectations, or habits, but simply because we genuinely want to do them.[12]

Having a busy life can make it easy for us to forget what's important to us, who we are, and what we used to enjoy doing. When you slow down and practice mindfulness you can uncover and remember these things. And once you remember, it is time to act and go for it. Having passion and desire for what we are doing leads to internal motivation and enjoyment.

Once I transitioned into pharmacy management, I discovered the importance of allocating time for my passions. I scheduled moments throughout my day to read for both pleasure and knowledge, jotting down and sharing what I learned, and exercising to maintain fitness and well-being. I also set aside time to explore museums and listen to music. Engaging in these activities gives me a sense of meaning and fulfillment.

There is one other aspect of self-discovery I want to share with you. Along with knowing your aptitudes and passions, it is the final essential element you need to uncover your authentic purpose in life. This element is referred to as your values.

If there is one aspect of your life, work, or a hobby that feels like it's really working for you, pay attention, focus on

---

12 Joan Didion, *The Year of Magical Thinking*, 2007.

it, and see where it leads. Once we start to figure out what we like to do and what we are skilled at, we should then consider what we should be doing. And that is doing what we value. We will discuss values in the next chapter.

In a nutshell: Having a passion means being deeply driven and emotionally connected to a specific interest, activity, or cause. It fuels your enthusiasm, motivates you to pursue it wholeheartedly, and brings immense joy and fulfillment to your life. Meaningful activities make us feel more alive and energized, providing something to look forward to. When you do something you believe in, you'll find passion.[13]

I think it is important to recognize that not everyone is fortunate enough to have a career that is also a passion. In my pharmacy management practice I was able to utilize my natural aptitudes and develop my skills by focusing on administrative tasks. This gave me a sense of fulfillment even if it never truly felt like my passion. Instead, I viewed it as the work that enabled me to afford and pursue my true passions outside of work.

13 Simon Sinek, "Where Passion Comes From," YouTube, 2020.

JOURNAL PROMPTS

- What do you love to do? If you could do anything, what would you do?
- When you are free to choose, how do you spend your time? What lights you up?
- What activities or subjects from work or school do you enjoy most?
- Do you have any aptitudes that you wished you had pursued and developed?
- Describe your ideal day, from waking up to going to sleep.
- Describe something you gave up—a job, a hobby, an instrument, or other activity. Why did you give it up? What would happen if you made the time and tried again?

RECOMMENDED RESOURCES
TO LEARN MORE ON THIS TOPIC

Book: *The Art of Work* by Jeff Goins

Video: *Where Passion Comes From* by Simon Sinek

Video: *Two Questions to Uncover Your Passion* by Noeline Kirabo

9. VALUES

*When your values are clear to you,
making decisions becomes easier.*
— ROY E. DISNEY

*I stand for honesty, equality, kindness, compassion,
treating people the way you want to be treated and helping
those in need. To me those are traditional values.*
— ELLEN DEGENERES

Values – your judgment of what behavior is important in life.

Identifying what is truly important to you in life is key to making decisions that align with your values. Living your values leads to you spending your time, energy, and money effectively. Values are your set of beliefs or standards that influence what you think and how you live your life. Knowing your values also gives you the strength and direction to carry on in difficult situations.

When we go through life without following our personal values, we can stray from our preferred path and lose our ability to generate real happiness, meaning, and success. Your values should be in harmony with your passions and aptitudes to complete your inner compass and make you resistant to manipulation or influence from outside sources, such as social media or people in positions of authority.

Studies have found that our personal values come from different sources. Family exerts the greatest influence on our value formation, while friends, peers, community, society, and education also play pivotal roles in shaping our value preferences. Values tend to be strong and long-lasting, but they can – and do – change over time.[14]

During adolescence, people often reject certain aspects of their upbringing as they explore and develop their own values and beliefs . This process involves moving from accepting things uncritically in childhood to rejecting them during adolescence and young adulthood, before eventually finding a balanced perspective that combines both influences. This dynamic process illustrates how values are not fixed but rather subject to growth and transformation throughout life.

From, my reading, here is a list of common values that people often consider important in their lives:[15]

- Financial independence or wealth
- Having freedom and independence
- Learning and knowledge
- Fun and adventure
- Good physical health and fitness
- Solid relationships and love of family
- Work accomplishments
- Honor, loyalty, and dependability

Other excellent principles include compassion, bravery, recognition, status, service, gratitude, and generosity. Your

14 Harry M. Kraemer Jr., From Values to Action, 2011.

15 Patrick King, The Art of Self-Awareness, 2022.

personal ethics and ideals may include many more virtues that motivate you.

Your most important four or five values are referred to as your core values. They express what you really believe about yourself, other people, life, and the world around you. To live an authentic life, you should never waiver on these. To follow your North Star or genuine self, always do the right thing for today and for your future. When your actions match your values, you can live a life that feels more meaningful, and decision-making is likely to become easier and feel more authentic.

Without considering your values, you will simply react to circumstances and make careless decisions that may hold you back in the long run. For example, let's say you're offered a job 60 miles farther away from home, and you quickly accept the offer because it will result in a nice salary increase. You assume the extra money will improve your life, without considering any other factors or implications. However, if two of your core values are family time and doing work you enjoy, you might end up with less of each. Soon, you will likely regret your decision.

How do you learn what values are important to you? It is helpful to listen to yourself and tune out all the other voices. It's said that we don't choose our core values; we clarify them. You can't pick a value that sounds good for you if it isn't something you truly care about. Use your mindfulness skills to contemplate and start a list of what you most value.

Living according to our values can be challenging. At times, it's simpler to create excuses that justify our negative actions, leading us to behave in ways that don't align with who we want to be. To prevent this, it helps to identify the external events that steer you off course from your values. These triggers prompt negative thoughts, feelings, and emotions, which, in turn, cause you to react in ways you might later regret.

For instance, a trigger for me is when someone criticizes me or points out my mistakes. In response, I often feel negative emotions and have a tendency to react strongly, momentarily gaining a sense of relief. However, this fleeting satisfaction is short-lived, and soon I find myself feeling regretful. Recognizing this, I understand the necessity of responding differently. I am committed to actively listening and trying to understand the criticism, aligning with my value of treating others kindly. I am working toward modifying my counterproductive response to this trigger and striving for a more constructive approach.

Once you have identified your core values, it becomes crucial to assess whether your actions consistently align with them. In general, a sense of self-satisfaction is more likely when our behavior resonates with our values, as opposed to when we act contrary to them. Here's an exercise designed to enhance your understanding of how you currently align with your core values and how you can incorporate additional behaviors that harmonize with them:

1. Begin with mindful introspection and journaling to explore how you presently express each of your core values. For instance, if one of your core values is to live with adventure, reflect on the activities that illustrate your adventurous spirit.

2. Next, think about whether you engage in any behaviors that contradict with your core values. For instance, if patience is a core value, consider if you sometimes snap at your children when they don't follow your instructions. Similarly, if humility is important to you, reflect on whether you frequently boast about your achievements. Aim to recognize instances where your behavior deviates from your values.

3. Lastly, ask yourself if there are fresh behaviors you could adopt to better align with your core values. For example, brainstorm ways to infuse more adventure,

patience, or humility into your daily routines and interactions.

Remember, this exercise is meant to foster self-awareness and growth. Be gentle with yourself and use it as an opportunity to make positive changes aligned with your values.

Living with integrity involves being truthful and consistent in your actions, aligning them with your values and beliefs. This requires staying dedicated, even when there's pressure to do otherwise. Achieving personal integrity requires self-awareness and a thorough exploration of your values. You must stick to this path and not stray from it. Sometimes, it takes courage to stand against peer pressure or the temptation of immediate benefits.

Suggestions on how you can develop personal integrity:[16]

- Help others without expecting something in return.
- Accept and listen to helpful criticism. *That's good advice for me.*
- Follow through on your commitments to show that you're reliable.
- Be transparent about things that are happening at home and at work.
- Use your time productively.

Consider the choices that have brought you feelings of pride and happiness. These are the decisions that align with your values. When choices feel like a compromise or make you uncomfortable, these are decisions that conflict with your values.

I'll end this section with the discussion of what I call *just-this-once* thinking. You might think to yourself "I know I shouldn't do this, but in this particular extenuating circumstance, *just-this-once,* it's not that big of a deal." It's easy to

---

16 Klare Heston, wikihow.com, 2022.

justify this way of thinking, but acting on it can start you down a path of cover-ups and lies.

Crossing a moral line, even once, removes a section of boundary, making it more likely you will do it again. Soon, there's no going back. The short-term reward you might get from crossing the boundary is not worth what it can ultimately cost you—a lost friend, a lost job, or even bankruptcy, divorce, or a jail sentence.

Just-this-once thinking can start with something that seems as innocuous as sharing confidential information with a friend, making a small alteration in a report to save time, or making a snide remark about a colleague. If you do happen to do this once, in a moment of weakness, you need to own up immediately to having made a mistake, as painful as that might be.

In a nutshell: Values represent the core principles and beliefs that guide your behavior and shape your decisions. They reflect what you consider important, define your sense of right and wrong, and serve as a compass for living a meaningful and authentic life. Living with integrity means that your values guide your decisions and actions, including what you eat and drink, what you buy, where you live, the work you do, the clothes you wear, and other choices. Always act true to who you say you are. Consider what you'd like people to say about your integrity when you're not around.

Now it's time to harness the power of self-knowledge gained from understanding your aptitudes, passions, and values, and take the next step toward uncovering your unique purpose. Living with purpose ignites a sense of control, deep satisfaction, and overall contentment propelling you to break free from stagnation and embrace a life of profound meaning and fulfillment. Get excited to explore the idea of purpose in the next chapter and discover its amazing insights!

JOURNAL PROMPTS

- What are some examples of integrity among your peers? How does it make you feel about that person?
- What are your values and in what ways do you live out these values every day?
- Feeling guilt or regret can come from a conflict between a personal value and a choice you made. What experiences have you had that made you feel guilt or regret?
- What values did you learn from your parents that you still hold as your values? What are the other sources of what you value?

RECOMMENDED RESOURCES TO LEARN MORE ON THIS TOPIC

Book: *The Values Factor* by John Demartini

Video: *Four Steps to Discovering Your Core Values* by Mckenzie Guzman Martinez

Video: *Personal Core Values* by Peace Itimi

10. PURPOSE

*Creating and integrating an empowering personal purpose
statement is one of the most important
investments we can make.*
— STEPHEN COVEY

*The mystery of human existence lies not in just staying alive,
but in finding something to live for.*
— FYODOR DOSTOYEVSKY

Purpose – the reason that something is done or created.
Your roadmap for life.

Meaningful – feeling that your life is significant, makes
sense, has value, and you are making a difference.

According to a 2018 analysis in the New York Times, only
around 25% of American adults say they have a clear sense
of what makes their lives meaningful. In today's busy lifestyle,
it's easy to get lost, not knowing how you got here, where you
are headed, or what you truly want to do. Many of us, including myself, did what we were told or what we thought was

expected of us, in our career choice, relationships, and how we lived our lives. People may have discouraged us from pursuing our dreams, telling us they weren't practical, or advising us to *follow the rules.*

However, despite following the rules, many of us feel like something is not right in our lives. This is likely because we didn't make authentic choices. We didn't consider our unique interests, abilities, or values when making decisions. We weren't aware of our true desires at the time. Now we feel disconnected, stuck, hopeless, or unmotivated.

Uncovering or figuring out your purpose is the final component and ultimate goal of self-reflection. It's something you need to know before you begin to plan and set suitable goals, which we will look at in Step 2. Without awareness of your purpose, even if you achieve your goals, you may not feel like you are making progress. Meaningful goals need to be aligned with a higher purpose.

The theory, Logotherapy, founded by a Holocaust survivor and psychiatrist Viktor Frankl, is founded on the belief that human nature is motivated by the search for a life purpose. A meaningful life is a long-term goal – not achieved in a day, week, or month, but over the years.

Viktor Frankl saw three sources of meaning in the camps: having significant work to do, loving and caring for another person, and having courage during difficult times.

Each of us must find our own path to fulfillment. Numerous people will try to influence your decisions and impose their ideas about what they think is best for you. They might try to direct you by putting up guardrails, speed limits, and caution signs. Consequently, you may find yourself driving with your foot on the brake. However, the better you know yourself and your desires, the less negative events beyond your control will upset you, derail you, or freeze you from moving forward.

Many of us go through life without discovering our purpose

or life mission because the process of self-discovery requires intentional effort. In reality, some people casually explore their life purpose, but usually not seriously until they encounter a so-called "midlife crisis" or experience a life-altering event or trauma. Such events may include divorce, job loss, becoming an empty-nester, serious health scares, or other distressing situations that prompt profound contemplation about the meaning of life.

A lack of purpose in life can lead to anxiety, depression and low self-esteem. Conversely, individuals with a sense of purpose tend to live longer, recover faster from illnesses, and are less likely to experience conditions like heart disease and Alzheimer's. The health benefits alone provide a compelling reason for people to seek meaning in their lives.[17]

Perhaps you can relate to Warren in the movie *About Schmidt,* portrayed by Jack Nicholson. Warren is a retired widower who spent his career in the insurance industry. During moments of introspection, he grapples with the feeling that he has wasted his life. He perceives that nothing he achieved during his decades of work will be useful to his much younger replacement. Additionally, he begins to believe that he failed as a husband and father because he devoted most of his time and energy to his job. Warren's story vividly illustrates the consequences of not having or following a purpose that values family. It serves as a stinging example of the emptiness that can arise without a clear sense of life's purpose.

Purpose serves as a personal compass, guiding you in the right direction when you encounter crossroads in life. A meaningful and strong purpose should revolve around benefiting others and making a positive difference in their world. It allows you to become part of something greater than yourself, reducing

---

17 Emotionmatters.co.uk, 2023

preoccupation with your own worries and anxieties.[18]

Having our own purpose is essential for all of us. For instance, in the PBS series *The Durrells in Corfu*, Louisa's purpose was to run the guesthouse and keep her family safe and well. Larry's was to change the world with a novel. Gerald's was to love and care for animals. One of the guests' purposes was to overthrow the government.

Revealing your purpose can take time, practice, and creativity. It requires having an open mind, being eager to learn, and engaging in serious reflection. Not all of us will be as fortunate as Jerry Seinfeld. In his book *Is This Anything*, Seinfeld describes how, at twenty years old, every neuron in his brain lit up when he walked into a comedy club for the first time. He felt like he had finally found his home on Planet Earth and knew his purpose. For most of us, discovering our passion takes more time and effort, but it is within us.

Having a purpose is like having a magical power. Once you uncover yours, be relentless and never stop pursuing it. It doesn't matter what happened yesterday; try even harder today. Having a purpose infuses you with energy and zest for life, leading to feelings of self-fulfillment and happiness. As Steve Harvey often said, "don't go through life with your brakes on." Knowing your purpose guides your decisions and motivates you to take action, as it answers the important question of *why do this*?

To attain *ikigai*, a Japanese word that roughly translates to "our reason for being," you must consciously choose your purpose. Ikigai is about looking inward and forward, in contrast to the word *meaning*, which relates to the feeling you have when looking backward at something you did. Having ikigai or purpose, and acting on it, will make your life feel meaningful, when you pause to reflect on your past actions.

---

18 Eloise Skinner, *The Purpose Handbook*, 2021.

If you have settled on several purposes, it may be helpful to choose the one that is most vital to your life at the moment and make that your primary purpose. The others can be considered secondary but still important purposes. Write them all out, read them, or say them out loud every day. This practice will help reinforce their significance in your life.

Being on purpose is similar to what athletes describe as *being in the zone,* as we explored in chapter three when discussing the state of flow. Being on purpose leads to feelings of flow and comes with several key feelings:[19]

- What you are doing feels effortless and fun.
- You feel energized and motivated.
- You have more courage and passion.
- You feel fully engrossed in what you are doing and lose track of time.
- You feel the joy of being on track.

Writing your purpose into a statement helps you internalize it in your mind and heart, and enables you to live it. This statement also can also be referred to as a personal mission statement, a motto, or a brand. Typically, it is one to two sentences long and can be structured like this:

To do [X Action] for [Y group of people] to
[have Z impact] with [optional: other details].

One example of a personal purpose statement, using this formula, is: "To lead fitness classes and workshops for busy professionals, enabling them to prioritize their health and wellness amidst demanding work schedules, promoting physical vitality and work-life balance."

---

19 Carol Adrienne, *Find Your Purpose, Change Your Life,* 2011.

The general consensus is that the following principles serve as a good foundation for writing your personal purpose statement:

- Keep them brief – one sentence is probably best, but two is fine.
- Keep them high level – a guiding charter that will hold up even as specifics change over time.
- Make it unique to you.

People with purpose have a clear sense of direction in life. They understand their deepest values, whether it's being a loving parent, supportive friend, a productive professional, or a contributing member of a community. They find satisfaction in setting relevant goals and making progress toward achieving them.

The desire to make progress on your purpose serves as a powerful motivator, driving you to jump out of bed in the morning and do your best. It can also provide a sense of calm during challenging times. Your purpose acts as a rudder, guiding you through life and keeping you on track toward your North Star. As the saying goes, "if you are passionate about what you do, you'll never work a day in your life."

Here are some other excellent examples of personal purpose statements:

- To inspire positive change through writing—using stories, personal experiences, and practical tips—to help people find joy and purpose in life. (Yes, that's mine.)
- Appreciate and enjoy family every day, by making decisions that put their best interests first.
- Acquire the knowledge needed to educate and empower individuals to achieve financial independence, enabling them to take control of their financial future.

- Create impactful materials, services, or products that empower girls and women to cultivate and sustain a healthy self-esteem.
- Work with and serve the elderly in a manner that fosters a sense of value, purpose, and belonging, ensuring they feel integral to a thriving society.

In a nutshell: Understanding your purpose is like having a compass for life, guiding you to make meaningful choices. When you know your purpose, you can create a strong plan that matches your values and dreams, pushing you toward a future full of happiness and achievement. Combining self-discovery with thoughtful planning sets the stage for a purpose-driven life that brings joy and positively impacts others. In the next step we'll look at planning and goals in more detail.

Keep at this process. Your purpose may change as you go through different stages of life. This doesn't mean you were wrong before; it simply means you've grown and gained new perspectives. Embracing this growth enables you to continuously align your actions with your evolving purpose, ensuring that you live a life that remains true to your authentic self.

As a word of caution, there are two easy ways to fail to live a purposeful life. The first is to let other people define it for you. The second is to be afraid to move forward. Neither approach helps you become the person you envision.

JOURNAL PROMPTS

- When you were a kid, what did you want to be when you grew up? Is that what you're doing now?
- When do you feel most like your authentic self?
- What do you do to help others? Do you think there is more you could be doing?
- Write a letter to yourself about what you believe is your true purpose in life, even if you haven't fully discovered it yet.

RECOMMENDED RESOURCES TO LEARN MORE ON THIS TOPIC

Book: *Man's Search for Meaning* by Viktor Frankl

Book: *The Happiness of Pursuit* by Chris Guillebeau

Book: *Life on Purpose* by Victor Strecher

Video: *How to Know Your Life Purpose in Five Minutes* by Adam Leipzig

Video: *What Is Your Purpose in Life* by Steve Harvey

PART III

STEP 2

Write an Action *Plan*

11. STARTING POINT

Choose a life that will keep expanding.
— ANN PATCHETT

You cannot go back and change the beginning, but you can start where you are now and change the ending.
— TERRY MCMILLAN

Starting point – a place that marks the beginning of a journey.

At certain moments in our lives, we have all experienced the feeling of being stuck. This state of being halts our progress and dampens our enthusiasm to pursue our goals and aspirations. We find ourselves entangled in indecision, plagued by worries and excessive overthinking. However, it is within our power to make a choice. We can either succumb to our current circumstances and remain trapped, or view this as a valuable learning opportunity to break free, regain momentum, and chart a new path toward a future brimming with possibilities.

Many of us set goals but then find ourselves stuck due to fear or self-doubt. Avoiding our fears only makes them grow and can end up controlling or limiting our lives. Instead, let's face our fears and take small steps to generate momentum. Don't let events from the past keep you from living in the present and moving forward. Focus on taking one small step to generate some momentum. Accept failures and setbacks as opportunities for learning and growth.

It is important to point out that nothing from your past should be an excuse to hold you back from reaching your goals or becoming who you truly want to be. We all need to push out negative emotions and beliefs about our limitations in order to free ourselves and rise above the rut.

In Step 1 you learned how to use mindfulness and journaling for greater self-awareness. You learned about your aptitudes, passions, and values. And you uncovered your inner North Star— your purpose. Before you determine your best path forward, you want to make sure you understand where you are starting from. Part of your self-understanding comes from identifying negative thoughts or limiting beliefs that are holding you in place.

The gap between your current position and your desired destination is what you need to bridge. In this chapter, we'll examine more about your current situation or starting point, helping you understand it better. We'll also discuss the obstacles that may be keeping you in place, and the challenges you may face as you begin your journey. If you're committed to making changes and moving forward, you'll need to take some risks and try new things, even if they feel uncomfortable at first.

Often, we find ourselves trapped in unproductive patterns due to limiting beliefs, old habits, or false assumptions. To break free, the first step is to take an honest and candid look at your current reality. Your truth should not be colored by wishful thinking or sounding good; it should reflect what it truly is at this very moment.

Get specific and pinpoint the real issues. What exactly is the problem? Why do you feel stuck? Perhaps you struggle to stick to a diet or exercise program, giving up after just a week or two. Take time to creatively explore the root cause of the problem. Focus on identifying issues that you have the power to change. Past failures may lead you to expect defeat even before you begin, but remember that this belief can be changed through learning and growth.

Once you find yourself in a mindful environment, take a moment to consider these thought-provoking questions. They will help you focus on your particular problem and uncover its root cause:

- What is the problem that I am experiencing?
- Why is this problem recurring? You want facts, not conjecture.
- Continue asking yourself *why* and keep drilling down to the root cause of the problem.

Once you feel certain you know the root cause, ask yourself why you think you haven't been able to fix the problem. What has been holding you back? We often feel stuck because we've lost sight of the bigger picture and what's important to us. Connect your goal to a bigger purpose, such as staying healthy and having more energy to play with your kids. Without such a strong reason for wanting to lose weight, it will be hard to sustain your diet or exercise routine.

Maybe you feel trapped because you chose a job for its great salary, not because it sounded like work you would enjoy. Or perhaps you felt unqualified to pursue a job in a field you were genuinely interested in. You eventually realize that the job you took is not a true reflection of your values, leaving you feeling out of sync with your life. Now, you're uncertain about how to improve your situation.

We often remain stuck because we don't see any way out of our current circumstances. However, keep in mind that there is no one perfect solution. Begin by making a list of any options you can think of, even if you're unsure about the necessary steps or resources required. Keep a positive mindset and think outside the box. Be willing to learn more about any option that seems plausible, even if you lack sufficient knowledge at the moment. In Step 3, you'll discover how to enhance the skills needed to break free from this feeling of being unstuck.

As we pursue our goals and aspirations, the concept of sacrifice inevitably comes into play. These moments of decision-making often involve difficult choices that can impact not only ourselves but also the lives of others. It's important to acknowledge that making changes in our lives may require letting go of certain things or compromising on certain aspects. This notion of sacrifice can evoke feelings of uncertainty and hesitation, as we weigh the potential consequences and consider the wellbeing of those involved.

However, while facing these challenges may not be easy, remaining stagnant or stuck can impede our personal growth and block us from fulfilling our true potential. Embracing change and being on purpose means making thoughtful choices that align with our core values and life vision.

By approaching sacrifice with empathy, open communication, and a deep commitment to our values and purpose, we can navigate these challenges more effectively. Be willing to adapt where necessary. Balancing our own desires with the needs and feelings of others allows us to strive for personal fulfilment, while also considering the impact on our relationships and connections.

In a nutshell: As we wrap up this chapter, let's recognize the importance of knowing our true starting point and the power of choice in shaping our future. Feeling stuck in our current situation is a common experience, halting our progress and dampening our enthusiasm. But we have the choice to either remain trapped or see it as a valuable opportunity for growth. By breaking free, regaining momentum, and charting a new path, we step into a future filled with abundant possibilities.

Now that you have a clearer picture of where you are now, let's explore where you want to go. A timeless piece of advice is, "Begin with the end in mind." So, before we talk about actionable steps along your path, we'll examine the impactful and inspiring practice of visualization, which helps you focus on what you want and where you want your journey to lead.

JOURNAL PROMPTS

- What is one thing you can work on today to start making progress?
- Describe your starting point. What are three things you feel grateful for and what is standing in the way of you moving forward?
- What are you afraid of? How can you confront those fears head on?
- Where do you feel out of alignment with the things that bring you joy?

RECOMMENDED RESOURCES TO LEARN MORE ON THIS TOPIC

Book: *Who Am I?* by the School of Life

Video: *Why Some of Us Don't Have One True Calling* by Emilie Wapnick

12. VISUALIZATION

Visualize your success, then take action.
— ANONYMOUS

Visualization is daydreaming with a purpose.
— BO BENNETT

Visualization – a technique involving focusing on positive mental images in order to achieve a particular goal.

Manifestation – the act or process of taking something hoped for and bringing it to life.

There is magic in thinking big! Choose to visualize with confidence and let your imagination soar. Envision your dream destination without holding back. Even if you have no idea how you'll get there, trust your instincts and believe that you'll figure it out. This is what some people refer to as "magical thinking," but it can be a powerful force.

In the last chapter, you identified your starting point, and now, let's consider where you want to go. There's a saying that everything happens twice. First in your mind, and then in reality. Your thoughts and beliefs have the power to shape your reality. While there may be exceptions, why not think big and see where it leads? By intensely focusing on what you want and imagining how it will feel when you achieve it, you'll create a path and make it happen.

Visualization and manifestation often receive a bad reputation for being seen as something mystical or supernatural, rather than grounded in reality. But the truth is, you don't need to be spiritual to benefit from these techniques. Anyone with a positive mindset, a little instruction, and a lot of persistence can do this.

Visualization is the powerful technique of vividly imagining your desired future, as if it's happening right now. It involves using all five senses of sight, smell, touch, taste, and hearing. By visualizing, you plant the seed of your goal deep in your subconscious, making your mind respond as if that desired outcome is already a reality in the present moment.

When visualizing, you want to think about where you want to end up and why. Setting and achieving goals becomes more challenging when you lack clarity about the purpose behind them. Genuine progress can only begin when you are certain about your destination and why it holds significance. Your goals should align with your purpose.

Effective visualizing also requires a mindset of experimentation, a thirst for learning, a mood of curiosity, and a willingness to be comfortable with the unknown. You must be prepared to open the next door even when you're uncertain where it leads. Having the courage and resilience to take risks is crucial. It requires the mindset of an explorer venturing into uncharted territories.

Here is a visualization process for you to start experimenting with. Let's imagine your vision for a new home:

1. Set aside dedicated periods of mindfulness, where you can sit uninterrupted for around 30-minutes and focus on defining your dream home.
2. Choose to either make an audio recording or write in your journal, depending on what works best for you. If you opt for recording, make sure you transcribe your thoughts later.
3. Before considering the details for your home, reflect on the "why" behind this dream home. How does it align with your purpose? Understanding the deeper significance of this vision will fuel your motivation.
4. Dream big! Imagine you have the opportunity to start anew and live anywhere you want, regardless of how wild or unrealistic it may seem at the moment.
5. Envision your perfect home. Feel what it's like to live there, visualize its location and how it looks both inside and out. Imagine who shares the home with you and your most cherished possessions. Picture your daily routine, including your work and the places you visit.
6. Contemplate the steps needed to realize this vision. Express gratitude for your good fortune and immerse yourself in the joy of achieving your dream.
7. Stay persistent. The timeline for turning your vision into reality is uncertain. While it won't be easy, having a meaningful purpose and self-belief will empower you to take the first steps toward making your dream home a reality.

Now, let's zoom out and ask ourselves some broader questions: What do I want to accomplish in my lifetime? What do I want to be remembered for? What truly makes my heart sing? If I could do anything in the world I wanted, what would that be?

If your vision includes a healthy mind and body, consider

setting a goal to exercise daily. Envision yourself as that individual who is already living this reality. Immerse yourself in the experience of working out every morning. See and feel yourself going through the motions with confidence, fulfillment, and peace. To establish this as a habit, start slowly and take small steps every day.

Allow yourself to dream and vividly see yourself living your vision. Through this process of visualization and manifestation, you'll begin to tap into the law of attraction. This law is a philosophy suggesting that positive thoughts bring positive results into a person's life, while negative thoughts yield negative results.

Focus on what you want, not what you don't want. Instead of dwelling on statements like "I hate being poor," shift your mindset to "I am working on my financial independence." By concentrating on the positive, you prevent the negative from taking hold of your mind, freeing yourself from its constraints.[20]

Stress stemming from negative thoughts can hinder your ability to focus on your vision. Stress often arises from dwelling on the past and reacting to past events, which distracts you from envisioning a brighter future. Resist the trap of victim thinking, as it will keep you firmly stuck in your current situation.

While reviewing your life's desires, don't let the initial lack of money, time, or energy deter you. Visualizing your achievement serves as the catalyst that enables the law of attraction to reveal ways to acquire these resources. Trust in the process, and you'll find that the universe aligns to support your journey toward your dreams.

I've read that when visualizing what you want, it's important to create space for it to happen. For instance, if your goal is to have a second car, consider building a larger garage to accommodate it. Similarly, if you want to hire another person to assist with your business, adding an extra desk can remove obstacles

---

20 Dr. Wayne W. Dyer, *The Power of Intention*, 2005.

and enhance your clarity. Reading your list of visions aloud daily, just as you do with your personal mission statements, also brings benefits. This repetition helps ingrain your desires into your subconscious, prompting it to actively work toward making them a reality.

A helpful way to focus on a vision is by creating a vision board or vision book, offering clarity on what achieving your goals will look like. One approach is to find pictures of people engaged in activities you aspire to do, and then display them on your board or paste them into a book. This visual representation serves as a reminder of what you are striving for.

To craft your vision board, you can purchase old magazines from resale shops and cut out images that align with your vision of the future. For example, if spending winters in a condo surrounded by palm trees in Florida is part of your dream, include such images. Be mindful and creative while crafting your visions; you can enhance the pictures by adding relevant words cutout from the magazine.

Consider forming a vision for each area of your life, such as career, relationships, home, health, and finances. If you prefer a digital approach, check out websites like canva.com for creating a digital vision board. Alternatively, compile your visions in a binder alongside your favorite motivational quotes to create a comprehensive vision book.

In a nutshell: As you continue to learn more about who you truly are—your values, your passions, your aptitudes, and your purpose—your vision will grow increasingly vivid and well-defined. Making progress toward your vision leads to a life of fulfillment, meaning, and success. My suggestion is to spend the majority of your day working on activities that truly resonate with your sense of purpose.

Once you have crafted your vision for the future, efficiently address minor issues that may pop up, and then refocus on what truly matters: pursuing your dream. Each present moment becomes an opportunity to take steps closer to your desired destination. A robust vision empowers you to pursue your dreams with unwavering enthusiasm and persistence.

Now that you understand your starting point and destination, it's time to devise a plan and set goals that will bridge the gap. But before proceeding, pause and engage with the following journal prompts and check out the recommended resources.

JOURNAL PROMPTS

- What would you still like to achieve in life? What have you achieved so far?
- What do your future home, work, family, and relationships look like? Why are these important to you?
- What does your life, well-lived, look like? What matters the most to you?
- What is one thing you can do today (or not do today) to help you be more on purpose?

RECOMMENDED RESOURCES TO LEARN MORE ON THIS TOPIC

Book: *Live Your Dream* by Joyce Chapman.

Video: *The Most Powerful Visualization Technique to Manifest Anything You Want in Life* by Mel Robbins

Video: *Visualization Step-by-Step Instructions* by Dr Weber Coaching

13. LONG-TERM GOALS

People are not lazy. They simply have impotent goals—
that is, goals that do not inspire them.
— TONY ROBBINS

You are never too old to set another goal
or to dream a new dream.
— C. S. LEWIS

Goal – the desired result that a person wants to reach or achieve.

Long-term goal – the end result. What you envision.

Now that we've explored the power of visualization, let's move on to the next step: goal-setting. Visualizing helps you dream big and imagine your desired future, but setting goals is what turns those dreams into reality. Goals reflect who you want to become, what you want to achieve, and what you want to have in life. They are your map to moving forward and making progress. Goals serve as the ladder to reach your vision.

Each goal should get you closer to reaching your vision.

Setting a goal answers the question of *what now?* In this section we will look at defining long-term goals, why they are important, and how to set them. Setting goals leads to personal development.

Setting clear and meaningful goals is essential because nothing significant happens without them. When you have well-defined goals, you're building a future that aligns with your potential and aspirations. It's about committing to the vision you've crafted through your visualizations.

In this chapter, we'll break down the process for setting long-term goals, understanding their importance, and learning how to set them effectively. Moving up each rung of the ladder brings you closer to living the life you envision.

Long-term goals are the big objectives that you aim to achieve, and they usually require more than a year to complete. In some cases, they might take much longer, like finding a cure for cancer. On the other hand, short-term goals, which we will look at in the following chapter, are more specific and have a shorter time frame, typically under one year. By breaking down a larger, long-term goal into several short-term goals, you can avoid procrastination and maintain focus on the task at hand.

I recommend setting at least one long-term goal for each area of your life, such as career, health, finance, relationships, fun, hobbies, and personal development. The only limits that exist are the ones you impose on yourself through your thinking or mindset.

Goals provide us with something to look forward to. Generally, people find true happiness when they are actively pursuing a goal that excites and energizes them. This is a key aspect of leading a fulfilling life. It's worth noting that you have already achieved many successes by reaching your goals, even if they were informal and not written out.

You have been successful in making friends, reading lengthy books, completing long drives, arriving at work on time, getting job offers after interviews, hearing a yes after asking someone out on a date, and even learning how to walk.

Only you can do this for yourself. Utilize your self-awareness, follow your heart, and listen to your instincts to choose goals that will bring you happiness, create self-fulfillment, and serve your purpose.

Long-term goals are developed through mindful reflection and journaling. As you contemplate what you want to achieve and the steps required to reach your vision, you identify the actions needed to bridge the gap between your current state and where you want to end up. Your goals should reflect your values and innermost convictions, serving as a source of motivation.

Here are some challenging examples of long-term goals: earning a management promotion in the next three to five years, completing a marathon two years from now, obtaining a degree within four years, achieving debt-free status, saving for retirement, becoming a better spouse or parent, and writing a book. This very book is the result of a long-term goal that took me over three years to accomplish.

Setting a powerful long-term goal involves:

- Ensuring that your strong long-term goal resonates with your aptitudes, passions, and values, reflecting your unique vision and purpose. It must be authentic and free from others' expectations of you.
- Making sure your goal relies on your actions, not factors beyond your control or luck.
- Anticipating potential obstacles and outlining strategies to overcome them.
- Not worrying if you don't have all the answers right away. Set the goal and figure out the necessary knowledge, skills, help, and resources later. Don't let limiting beliefs hold you back from thinking big.

• Putting your goal in writing and displaying it where you can see it daily. This focused reminder fuels your heart and mind. Consider adding a picture to your vision board that illustrates the achievement of your goal, such as your family in front of your dream home with the expected moving-in year.

Goals should hold personal meaning to you; otherwise, as the novelty wanes and effort remains, motivation dwindles. Progress toward meaningful goals boosts confidence and empowers you to set new, seemingly unimaginable ones.

Avoid getting stuck in the *messy middle* of reaching a goal by resisting the urge to give up. This obstacle may occur many times as you move up the ladder. Starting is easier than staying resilient and maintaining your progress. It's important to not always expect fun, fast, and easy. I recommend taking slow, manageable steps to get past the messy middle. An incomplete action can become a major source of stress and anxiety.

You also want to realize you might ultimately fail at some of your goals or that your goals might change over time. But don't let that possibility stop you from pushing forward now. Aristotle says, and I paraphrase, *we are happy only when we are making progress toward something that we truly want.* Every time you complete a task, your brain releases endorphins that create a sense of wellbeing. The bigger the task, the greater the amount of endorphins.

Understand your intention clearly in order to define your desires. Not everyone requires grand aspirations; a dream could be as simple as securing a Monday through Friday job to preserve family time. Learning to cook might be your long-term goal to enhance your household contributions. Depending on your current commitments and availability, the time it takes to achieve these goals could vary, so be patient and persistent.

A loftier long-term ambition could be finishing college.

Perhaps you had to stop because you were too far in debt and could no longer qualify for the additional loans you needed to finish. Or you had to step away to take care of elderly parents, or go to work to support their financial needs. Regardless of the scale of your aspiration, having a long-term goal not only fuels your personal growth and self-esteem, but also serves as testament to your resilience and determination in the face of challenges.

Take control of your goals, visions, and dreams; don't leave them to chance. Imagine yourself decades from now, reflecting on your journey. You wouldn't want to be left wondering, "How did I get here?" Your intentional actions today shape the path toward your future.

In a nutshell: Effectively establishing goals for your future necessitates ongoing reflection on your past. Assume the roles of both consultant and the client, probing where you want to go and how you can get there. Long-term goals should harmonize with your aptitudes, passions, values, and purpose, ensuring sustained motivation even when the complexities of life threaten to disrupt your path.

Maintain a delicate equilibrium between taking on too many goals and having too few. If you are already busy and start considering a new goal, jot it down on a future bucket list. Conversely, if you find yourself feeling bored and seeking distractions, it may be a sign that you need to set more goals or add some risk to challenge yourself with your existing goals. Also, if you are feeling stuck, use your imagination to decide if your goals match your purpose.

Keep in mind that it's easy for the expectations of a goal to exceed the actual outcome, often due to a lack of a focused plan. To avoid disappointment, break significant goals into smaller, manageable ones that feel realistic. In the next chapter, we'll discuss making plans and setting short-term goals.

JOURNAL PROMPTS

- What goals have you achieved in the past? What did you learn from them?
- What are five long-term goals that you want to reach? Be specific.
- What is the main reason you want to achieve each goal? What is your 'why'?
- What are five possible things that could get in the way of meeting one of your specific long-term goals?

RECOMMENDED RESOURCES TO LEARN MORE ON THIS TOPIC

Book: *Goals!: How to Get Everything You Want* by Brian Tracey

Book: *Breakthrough Goals!* by A. K. Spencer

Video: *How to Find Your Long-term Goals* by Carl Pullein

14. SHORT-TERM GOALS / PLANNING

Planning is bringing the future into the present
so that you can do something about it now.
— ALAN LAKEIN

Good planning without good working is nothing.
— DWIGHT D. EISENHOWER

Short-term goal – what you need to do to reach your long-term goal; how you will get there.

Strategy – a plan of action designed to achieve a long-term goal. Guides our choices on how to use our limited resources.

Planning – visualizing an activity and defining it step by step.

Many people make excuses for staying stuck and making little progress with their long-term goals. Common reasons include viewing the goal as too complicated, uncertainty about where to start, harboring limiting beliefs or self-doubt, and falling into the trap of self-sabotage driven by fear of failure and procrastination. These negative thoughts and feelings become significant obstacles to goal achievement.

Now that you have set your long-term goals, it's time to shift our focus to the next step: developing a plan or strategy to reach them. This involves breaking down the seemingly daunting long-term goals into several manageable short-term goals. These specific and actionable intentions not only help you stay focused but also provide a way to measure your progress and growth. Short-term goals are typically achievable within a timeframe of less than 12 months.

As the old adage puts it, if you fail to plan, you plan to fail. A short-term goal is a detailed plan designed to move you closer to reaching a long-term destination. It serves as a strategic roadmap to keep you moving forward and allows for continuous improvement through small adjustments along the way.

Short-term goal setting holds significant value for four important reasons:

1. Short-term goals are more motivating, providing a sense of accomplishment and progress.
2. They make the overall process feel more manageable by breaking down the journey into achievable steps.
3. They give you a clear action plan, outlining the specific tasks and actions required.
4. They allow for regular reflection and adjustments, enabling you to stay on track and adapt as needed.

As I learned in a business management class, setting goals is essential for getting things done and effectively managing progress. Without well-formulated goals, making significant strides or achieving success becomes challenging. Well-defined goals help you stay organized and enhance productivity.

Before writing your short-term goals, take some time to review the long-term goal for clarity and recommit to it.

Remind yourself why you want to achieve this goal and how it fits into your vision for the future.

To create short-term goals that feel tangible and motivating, employ the SMART method.[21] The mnemonic stands for:

- **S** – Specific: the goal needs to be detailed and precise.
- **M** – Measurable: there must be a clear way of measuring whether or not you've attained the goal.
- **A** – Attainable: the goal needs to be realistic (but challenging).
- **R** – Relevant: the goal needs to lead toward your broader objectives.
- **T** – Timebound: there should be specific deadlines for achieving your goal.

Here are a couple of examples demonstrating the use of the SMART method:

1. **To eliminate credit card debt:** I will pay the outstanding balance of $5,000 on my credit cards in installments and become debt-free within thirty-six months. I may be able to achieve this quicker by negotiating with each credit card company to reduce my interest rate. Then, I'll systematically pay off the card with the highest interest rate down to the lowest interest rates.
2. **To improve my health:** I will be able to do ten consecutive pull-ups and fifty push-ups three months from today to increase my strength. I will achieve this by training on my own at the gym every third day and also meeting with a personal trainer once per month to guide my progress.

---

21 George T. Moran, *There's a S.M.A.R.T. to Write Managements' Goals and Objectives*, 1981.

You should be able to identify each element of the SMART method in these two goals. Now, try writing a SMART goal for each of your long-term goals.

Other experts suggest using the 3P format – positive, present, and personal. This is a way of writing goals as if we have already accomplished them. A lot of athletes do this type of mental rehearsal to envision what it will feel like to have won.[22]

It's possible to combine the SMART method and 3P format when writing your plans. Here is one example:

I am relieved to have paid off my $5000 credit card balance. I accomplished this by negotiating with each credit card company to reduce my interest rate and routinely making thirty-six monthly installments. I systematically paid off the card with the highest interest rate down to the lowest interest rate.

Here are a few additional planning tips to enhance your effectiveness in reaching your goals:

- Start with small early activities in your plan to build confidence.
- Write down your plan and keep it where you can see it frequently.
- Stay optimistic and take action right away.
- Seek inspiration from success stories of others who have achieved similar goals.
- Include measurement elements in your plan, such as pounds lost, dollars saved, or pages written.
- Acknowledge potential obstacles and have a contingency plan in place. Don't let a failure of imagination hold you back.[23]
- Set a deadline or target date range that allows for some flexibility.

---

22 Brian Tracy, *Goals!*, 2010.

23 James Clear, *Atomic Habits*, 2018.

- Remember that planning is an ongoing process. Review your plan and progress monthly, and be ready to make changes or create new plans as needed.
- Share your plan with an accountability partner to stay on track and motivated.
- Celebrate each completed activity and experience the rewarding dopamine release as you check it off on your planner.

Having a positive mindset when envisioning the future is motivating and encourages us to take the necessary steps to achieve our goals—but only if we consider and account for potential obstacles along the way.[24]

Have you ever postponed pursuing important goals or dreams because you couldn't find the time, energy, or money to go after them? If that's the case, today is the day to start making a plan with short-term goals that will help you save money, harness your energy, and free up time to make progress toward your significant goals.

In a nutshell: Throughout this chapter, we confronted common excuses that hinder progress toward our long-term goals. From complexity and uncertainty to self-doubt and fear, these barriers can impede our journey. However, we discovered that with clear goals, actionable plans, and a positive mindset, we can overcome these obstacles.

Keep in mind that the planning question of "What now?" can be a moving target. Don't dwell on sudden changes to your plan due to failures or setbacks. Instead, stay aware of the need to adjust your approach from time to time.

Successful people fail to reach their goals far more often than unsuccessful people because they never give up until

---

24 Gabriele Oetttingen, *Rethinking Positive Thinking*, 2015

they achieve success. They accept a failure, learn from it, and continue to progress. You can do the same if you desire the result intensely enough. Stay devoted to your purpose.

As we move forward, we'll explore the advantages of using a monthly planner. It is an important tool to effectively allocate our time and enhance our efficiency. I'll guide you through the process and provide practical tips for turning your aspirations into daily actions. So, get yourself a monthly planner and a pen because it's time to take another empowering step toward achieving your dreams.

JOURNAL PROMPTS

- What are good long-term and short-term plans for advancing in your current career or for changing careers?
- What long-term and short-term goals should you include to save for your emergency fund, future retirement, car, or vacation?
- What long-term and short-term goals can you articulate to maintain motivation for a sustainable exercise plan?

RECOMMENDED RESOURCES TO LEARN MORE ON THIS TOPIC

Book: *Your Best Year Ever* by Michael Hyatt

Book: *One Small Step Can Change Your Life* by Robert Maurer

Video: *Setting SMART Goals* by Better Than Yesterday

15. DAILY STEPS / DAILY PLANNER

The secret of getting ahead is getting started.
— MARK TWAIN

You don't have to see the whole staircase,
just take the first step.
— MARTIN LUTHER KING

Process – a series of actions or steps taken in order to achieve a particular end.

Action steps – specific efforts, tasks, or actions that are done to reach a goal.

A daily planning calendar is an actionable tool that can save you many hours per week, if you use it correctly. Each day presents a new opportunity to get organized, make progress on your plan, and get closer to reaching your goals. In the previous two chapters you learned about setting long-term and short-term goals. This chapter will discuss a third type of goal: daily goals. Daily goals are where the rubber meets the road. They are the actionable steps you take to reach your short-term goals on your journey toward achieving your long-term goals.

Expecting too much too fast can lead to less progress and a higher chance of giving up. This may explain why so many people fail to stick to New Year's resolutions. Rapid changes without a structured plan often result in slipping back into old habits as your enthusiasm quickly fades.

Achieving a big goal is a journey that, with the right attitude and a focused plan, can lead you to success. Using a daily planner to outline your tasks for each day helps contribute to an organized approach, clarifying your daily objectives.

Sustained progress starts with taking one step today and one more tomorrow. Each small step builds energy, confidence, and a sense of pride, motivating you to keep moving forward. Success is the culmination of small, incremental gains sustained over time.

You don't want to be a spectator of your life; you want to be in control. Procrastinating will only decrease the likeliness of taking action. However, by completing small daily steps, you can lay the foundation for significant success—even achieving things you never thought possible.

The best way I have found to plan and focus my daily activities is to use a planner. I use the Professional 8.5 x 11 Weekly/Monthly Planning Calendar sold at many office supply stores and specialty shops. Since I like to carry mine around, I prefer one that provides a few pages for making notes on ideas that pop into my head and that I don't want to forget. There are dozens of different styles available for you to choose from.

You might be aware of the basics of using a planner, but I will explain how I use mine and the benefits I enjoy from using it. I like to include a few actions steps each week for making progress on each of my goals. I include steps for goals in my career, relationships, budgeting and investing, self-care, having fun, and other areas of life I am focused on developing.

This week I might be working on these six goals:

1. Progressing with my manuscript to meet the deadline for sending it off for editing in three months.
2. Engaging in reading for research and pleasure to enhance my knowledge, skill and enjoyment.
3. Effectively managing my income and expenses to achieve my monthly savings targets.
4. Prioritizing exercise five days per week to ensure good health and well-being.
5. Executing a couple of marketing activities to further develop my publishing business.
6. Arranging a game night with friends or enjoying a comedy movie for light-hearted moments filled with laughter.

I also like to schedule time on most days for one cultural or sporting activity. That could include watching a documentary, going to a play, visiting a museum, or playing pickleball. An example of one day from my planner might look like this:

5:00–5:30	Wake up. Turn on the coffee maker. Review plans for today and make adjustments if necessary
5:30–6:30	Mindful journaling (include expressions of gratitude)
6:30–7:30	Eat breakfast, check email, budgeting and banking
7:30–8:15	Exercise, shower, and dress
8:15–11:00	Writing session
11:00–12:00	Eat lunch
12:00–1:30	Meet friend or colleague at the art museum
1:30–3:30	Marketing activities for my business
3:30–5:30	Reading a chapter or two from my ongoing books
5:30–9:00	Dinner with my wife. Game night or a comedy movie
9:00–9:30	Journaling and then bedtime (it has been a meaningful day)

This is just one example, and the schedule can vary from day to day. As seen in the above schedule, sometimes it's possible to combine two activities into one, like I did between 12:00 and 1:30pm, by taking action steps in both maintaining a relationship and enjoying a cultural activity. Additionally, I include prompts in my planner for drinking several glasses of water daily, simplifying the monitoring of my hydration goal.

In addition to my paper planner, I also like to enter events and appointments in my iPhone calendar to receive reminders. Each evening, when writing out my planner schedule for the next day, I check my phone calendar to make sure I include these appointments and avoid overbooking myself. This dual approach helps me stay organized and ensures I never miss important commitments.

You may find—like I do—that taking time each morning or evening to complete your planner for the next day works for you. Alternatively, you might prefer planning out your entire week on Sunday. Experiment with different methods to see what suits you best. It's all about finding a planning routine that fits your preferences and helps you stay organized and focused on your goals.

On days that I work at the pharmacy, my shift takes up a significant portion of my day. However, I still make sure to schedule shorter activities for my other goals. For example, I dedicate just 30 minutes each to exercising, journaling, writing, answering messages and emails, and reading. For me, taking a small step toward my goals is much better than taking no step at all.

You can get creative in making your planner work for you. The aesthetics don't matter, and neither does perfectly checking off each daily task. Your planner isn't meant to look perfect, just as you are not meant to be perfect. So, put your energy into using your planner for scheduling and making progress, without any expectations of perfectionism.

The only personal information I include in my planner is my name and email address. Keeping information such as usernames, passwords, PINs, addresses, and phone numbers in your planner may compromise your personal data if it were ever to get lost or stolen.

Be selective about adding an activity to your schedule, but then make an effort to adhere to it. Don't give up your lunch break to catch up on a work project. In fact, if possible, take a short walk out in the fresh air after you eat. Also, avoid staying late at work to clear your email when you had planned to exercise, or when your family is anticipating your presence for dinner. Be deliberate in how you manage your time.

Importantly, each activity on my calendar represents progress toward a short-term goal that aligns with a long-term goal. I perform progress reviews at the end of each day, week, month, and year. What got done, what didn't, why, and should I keep it as a step or goal?

The use of a daily planner offers numerous benefits:

- It keeps you organized and aids in time management.
- It holds you accountable for completing your planned tasks.
- You can set up recurring weekly themes on specific days, such as dedicating every Monday from 9am to 10am for *Goal Setting*.
- It promotes good mental health by preventing feelings of being overwhelmed, stressed and anxious, while also avoiding the fear of forgetfulness.
- It can also positively impact your physical health by tracking diet, exercise, and medical appointments.
- Financial health improves as you include reminders for bill payments and regular savings contributions.
- It allows for creativity, with options like adding stickers, pictures, quotes, or poems.

- You can track activities and interactions to schedule them again, ensuring a balanced social life.
- It serves as a reminder to focus on your long-term goals and purpose. Align your daily and weekly goals to achieve these objectives.
- It encourages mindfulness and journaling, facilitating the scheduling of activities that boost happiness and well-being.

In a nutshell: I recommend using your daily planner to strive for a balanced life. Many of us tend to focus solely on work and neglect progress on our other goals. By scheduling a variety of activities in your planner, you can avoid being too one-sided. I suggest starting each day with a little scheduled time to express gratitude for the opportunities that lie ahead and for visualizing the progress you will make. Make it a habit by writing it in your planner.

In the next chapter, we will look at additional strategies to enhance your time-management skills and further ensure you accomplish all your daily steps and activities.

JOURNAL PROMPTS

- Review your long-term and short-term goals. What activities do you need to work on this week? Divide them up by days of the week. For each activity, note which goal they are helping you achieve.
- What were the biggest mistakes you made this week?
- How do you feel about your physical health? What is one thing you can do to improve it this week?
- How much time do you spend watching TV or browsing social media?

RECOMMENDED RESOURCES TO LEARN MORE ON THIS TOPIC

Web search: look at office supply stores or personal development sites and find yourself a daily planner that suits your taste and order it today. You already have a journal, right?

Book: *Plan Your Day* by N. Bowen

Video: *How to Actually Use Your Planner* by Alaina from The Organized Money

16. TIME MANAGEMENT

Where your attention goes, your time goes.
— IDOWU KOYENIKAN

You can't make up for lost time.
You can only do better in the future.
— ASHLEY ORMON

Golden hours: *Every morning I am handed 24 golden hours. They are one of the few things in this world I get free of charge. If I had all the money in the world, I could not buy an extra hour. What will I do with this priceless gift? I must use it as it is given only once. Should I waste it, I can never get it back.*
— ANONYMOUS

Time management - the ability to plan and control how one spends the hours in a day to effectively accomplish one's goals.

Fritter away – to waste or squander something, usually in a foolish way.

When something holds importance to you, you'll always find time for it. However, if you often feel overwhelmed by the day's activities and struggle to accomplish your planned tasks, it's crucial to assess how you spend your time and work on improving your time management skills. If you don't have a clear purpose for doing something, staying busy with it is a waste of time. Time management is about effectively managing your activities.

For activities to be truly meaningful, they should contribute to your personal growth and help you reach your full potential. Regrettably, research shows that most people utilize only a fraction of their potential, as they invest a considerable amount of time in activities that don't add value to their lives.[25] A prime example of this is the excessive amount of time spent on screens, which often consumes several hours per day for many individuals. We remain busy but achieve very little, chasing instant stimulation and dopamine rushes. For the great majority of us, this habit provides no long-term benefits and merely squanders our precious time.

Fortunately, time management is a learnable skill that can be improved. By using your time wisely, you acknowledge that it's a limited and valuable resource, and making the most of it becomes vital. Procrastination and distraction must be overcome, as they have detrimental effects on your happiness and overall satisfaction with life. Each moment presents a choice on how to use your time: to engage in this activity or that one? By mastering excellent time management skills, you can strike a healthy balance between your professional and personal life.

Recognize that your time is your own, but preserving its ownership requires effort and determination. Apart from wasting time on screens, many of us engage in activities that might not contribute to our goals. This often occurs at work when we struggle to delegate effectively or find it challenging

---

25 Jon Acuff, *Finish*, 2018.

to say no when asked to participate in extra projects.

Throughout each day, we must be mindful and intentional to resist impulsive behaviors. When sudden urges arise, pause and reflect before taking action. Question whether the action, or inaction, helps you to reach your goals. Doing the right thing demands effort. Making progress toward your goals often means accepting short-term discomfort and saying no to strong desires. Make wise choices.

Here are ten counterproductive habits that can consume valuable time during your day:

1. Email
2. Phone calls
3. Text messages
4. Social media
5. Internet surfing
6. Being a perfectionist
7. News alerts
8. Noisy environment
9. Talking with co-workers
10. Procrastination

Improving your time management skills will boost your confidence and effectiveness in both your work and personal life. Each day's end will bring a profound sense of purpose as you make significant strides toward your goals. With better time management, you'll have more quality time for your loved ones, friends, and self-care. This will lead to improved physical and mental well-being, leaving you feeling better overall.

Based on my reading and personal experience, I've discovered that the way you begin your mornings can significantly influence the rest of your day. When you establish focused, productive, and successful morning routines, you create a foundation for a day filled with similar positive outcomes. Moreover, the improvements you make in your morning habits can have a ripple effect, positively impacting other areas of your life, leading to overall fulfillment and success.[26]

For example, I've noticed that my early morning discipline sets the tone for making healthier choices throughout the day. I feel more motivated to engage in regular exercise, maintain balanced nutrition, and prioritize self-care, which directly enhances my overall health. Also, approaching the day with purpose and joy can be inspiring to those around you, creating a chain reaction of optimism and motivation.

I suggest starting your morning with mindfulness. Reflect on your purpose and goals, visualize how you want your day to unfold, read a self-help article, or listen to a short motivational podcast. You'll likely gain valuable insights, so keep your planner or journal nearby to jot down notes.

Here are some effective time management suggestions to help you take control of your days:

1. Stay aware of how you spend your time by keeping an activity log in 15-minute intervals for a week. This will reveal unproductive time usage.
2. Visualize your goals for motivation and imagine how achieving them will bring positive changes. Consider the feelings associated with accomplishing those goals.
3. Be confident in your choices and stick to your set deadlines for achieving goals. Review your progress daily and adjust your approach if necessary.
4. Get organized and maintain that organization to avoid wasting time searching for misplaced items. It's a more efficient use of your valuable time.
5. Delegate tasks when possible. Seek help and advice from others, which not only lightens your workload

---

26 Hal Elrod, *The Miracle Morning*, 2012

but also allows them to develop their skills and confidence.

6. Utilize any downtime productively. Accomplish tasks while waiting for appointments or meetings to start.
7. When you catch yourself procrastinating, reflect on what you're avoiding and the underlying thoughts and feelings causing the delay.
8. Focus on one thing at a time. Attempting to multitask consumes time and energy, as the human brain is not efficient at handling multiple activities simultaneously.
9. Maintain your energy levels through regular exercise, a healthy diet, and sufficient sleep.
10. Reward yourself when you complete your planned steps. Treat yourself to a movie or low-carb beer for small achievements and consider a larger reward for major goal accomplishments.

In our fast-paced world, mastering time management is a valuable skill that can significantly enhance your productivity and overall wellbeing. There are numerous personal benefits to refining your time management skills. People who practice effective time management techniques often experience the following:

- increased productivity;
- more energy to accomplish tasks;
- reduced stress;
- more free time for personal activities;
- greater task completion;
- improved relationships with others; and
- enhanced self-esteem.

In a nutshell: In essence, time management involves prioritizing meaningful activities over aimless drifting and recognizing the importance of execution for success. It's crucial to make the most of the 24 hours we have each day.

In the upcoming final chapter of Step Two – Happiness and Living a Balanced Life, we will explore how to use our time to develop a more balanced life and what it truly means to find happiness.

JOURNAL PROMPTS

- What are the distractions stealing your time? What is going on in your mind that is making it tough to focus?
- What time of day do you feel most productive or unproductive?
- What does being productive look like for you? Describe your ideal day of productivity in detail.
- What did not go well today? How can you make it better tomorrow?

RECOMMENDED RESOURCES TO LEARN MORE ON THIS TOPIC

Book: *The Time Management Solution* by Damon Zahariades

Book: *Time Management for the Overwhelmed* by Violet Mendez

Video: *Time Management – Ten Productivity Tips and Tricks That Work* by Philip VanDusen

17. HAPPINESS AND LIVING A BALANCED LIFE

Balance isn't something you achieve "someday".
— NICK VUJICIC

You will never be truly satisfied by work until you are satisfied by life.
— HEATHER SCHUCK

Balanced Life – determining what is most important to you and expending your time and energy accordingly.

Happiness – positive emotions and life-satisfaction; subjective wellbeing.

Living a balanced life is a key part of healthy living. By managing your time and energy wisely, you nurture all aspects of yourself—body, mind, and spirit. This often entails embracing tasks that are difficult and challenging, as they contribute to personal growth and flourishing. However, it's important to acknowledge that achieving greatness in one area might necessitate sacrifices in other aspects of life, as discussed in Chapter 11.

It is said, "If you want to become the best at one single thing, you have to sacrifice everything else." Just think about professional athletes or world-class musicians and what they had to give up to reach the pinnacle of their fields. It's true that not everyone may be willing to make such a trade-off and become single-focused in their pursuit of ambitions. Moreover, living in such a manner raises an important question: Once that one thing is over, who are you then? Is it truly worth sacrificing your health or relationships to become an overachiever?

Balanced living means considering all components of life that are important to you, often visualized as the Wheel of Life.[27] The spokes on this wheel represent various aspects including:

1. Business and career – includes your vocation, work, motherhood, fatherhood, parenting, volunteering, leadership, and future planning such as retirement.
2. Finances – budgeting, savings, investments, and financial security fall into this category.
3. Health and fitness – prioritizing your overall wellbeing, both physical and mental health.
4. Family and friends – fostering meaningful connections with loved ones and contributing positively to your community and social life.
5. Main relationship – nurturing your dating life, intimate relationships, and life partnership.
6. Personal development – embracing lifelong learning, exploring art and culture, fostering creativity, and focusing on self-development, spiritual growth, achieving potential, and finding meaning in life.
7. Fun and recreation – setting aside time for leisure, pursuing hobbies, engaging in sports, and finding enjoyment in various activities.

---

27 Charles Hobbs, *Time Power*, 1988

8. Physical environment – ensuring a comfortable and secure home or work-from-home space.

Taking care of each of these spokes in your life's wheel is crucial for maintaining balance and overall well-roundedness. By dedicating attention to these essential areas, you can lead a more fulfilling and harmonious life.

Most people tend to dedicate the majority of their time to the business and career spoke, especially during their working years. In my experience, I discovered that reducing my work hours significantly contributed to achieving a better balance in how I distributed my time. However, regardless of your life stage, it's essential to strive for a reasonable balance in the various spokes of life that hold significance for you. One effective method to achieve this is by utilizing your daily planner to schedule dedicated blocks of time for each key component of life.

Learning to allocate your time, energy, talent, and financial resources in a manner that aligns with your long-term priorities and intentions is crucial. By doing so, you ensure that you are investing in what truly matters to you. It's also important to recognize that life is dynamic and ever-changing. Therefore, you always have the flexibility to adjust your choices and activities along each spoke, to cater to your evolving needs and aspirations. Using this adaptable approach empowers you to lead a fulfilling and balanced life that remains in sync with your desires and objectives.

According to Dr. Diana Aguiar Vieira, "the key to happiness is a balanced life."[28] After coming across this statement, I felt compelled to learn more about the concept of happiness. What I learned is that while happiness can be achieved through various experiences in life, the true

---

28 Diana Aguiar Vieria, "Balance is the new happy", Marialma.com, 2019.

essence lies in finding meaning and purpose in what we do.

While the pursuit of happiness is natural, it's often the pursuit of meaningful goals and actions that leads to the emergence of true happiness as a byproduct. When we engage in activities that align with our values and aspirations, we are more likely to experience genuine happiness and contentment. Therefore, it is crucial to focus not solely on the pursuit of happiness as a singular goal, but rather on seeking meaningful experiences and connections.

From my reading, I came across compelling evidence that sheds light on the different factors contributing to our overall happiness:[29]

- 50% of our baseline happiness is determined by genetics, passed along from our parents and ancestors.
- 10% is influenced by life circumstances, such as childhood experiences, social and financial status, and overall health.
- 40% is within our control, comprising our attitudes, mindset, daily choices, and actions.

The remarkable aspect is that this 40% is entirely in our hands. By acting with purpose and intention, we can increase our feelings of happiness. However, achieving this requires sincere effort and commitment from each one of us.

According to a recent Gallup poll, worldwide unhappiness has increased steadily from 24% in 2006 to 33% in 2021. Happiness is derived from experiences of joy, contentment, or positive wellbeing, combined with a subjective sense that one's life is good, meaningful, and worthwhile. It's important to understand that no one can be happy all the time; happiness is a complex and dynamic emotion.

---

29 Sonja Lyubomirsky, *The How of Happiness*, 2008.

Numerous authors concur that happiness is not a fixed destination but rather a journey toward a purposeful and meaningful life. By setting goals aligned with your sense of purpose, you will find happiness as you progress along your path.

Additionally, learning to appreciate what you already have can lead to greater happiness, rather than constantly yearning for more. The pursuit of material possessions can bring about added concerns and stress related to potential risk, damage, or loss.

Many of the things we believe will bring happiness and fulfillment often provide only temporary satisfaction. Avoid falling into the trap of thinking that achieving certain dreams, such as a work promotion, having a baby, buying a bigger boat, or purchasing a house, will lead to lasting happiness. Instead, view happiness as something attainable through engaging in activities that you love and enjoy, which also benefit others, rather than relying on material possessions or accomplishments solely for personal gain.

Temporary satisfaction or happiness is further defined in a psychological idea referred to as the *hedonic treadmill*. It explains how people get used to changes in their lives and return to their usual level of happiness over time. It means that no matter if something good or bad happens, we eventually go back to feeling the same as before. So, again, seeking happiness through external things like money or possessions might give us a temporary boost, but it won't last long. Instead, we should focus on gratitude, personal growth, and meaningful relationships for lasting happiness.

As a fitting example of how seeking happiness from external sources can be short-lived, let me share a story about a service-provider I know. He once expressed immense pride and happiness when he finally purchased the boat of his dreams, believing it would make him feel good about himself. However, the initial joy soon turned into frustration as he found himself overwhelmed with the amount of work required to make the boat meet his expectations. Even before he could set sail, his enthusiasm dwindled as he started comparing his boat to larger and newer ones docked at his marina. Rather than bringing him happiness, the purchase seemed to create more anxiety and discontentment. He began to believe that owning one of those bigger, shinier boats would truly make him happy.

Another trap to avoid is convincing yourself that you can't be happy because of the challenges you've faced, such as divorce, job loss, or a stock market drop. It's not the events themselves that dictate your happiness; rather, it's your response to them that shapes your future. Therefore, choose your response thoughtfully, and refrain from engaging in negative self-talk like, "If only I had made different decisions in the past, I would be happy today."

Mahatma Gandhi once said, "The best way to find yourself is to lose yourself in the service of others." Giving back is a significant aspect of finding happiness, as it activates the reward center in our brains. Even, if you can't give financially, offering your time can be equally meaningful.

While there is no magic formula for happiness, certain key factors can be prioritized in your daily life to enhance your overall well-being. Most researchers highlight common themes such as cultivating gratitude, having strong relationships, being present in the moment, and taking care of your mental and physical health.

One way to incorporate these themes or factors is through gratitude visualization. Simply take a few minutes each day to find a quiet moment, close your eyes, and reflect on the things you are grateful for. Vividly picture these aspects in your mind, whether it's the people you love, your proudest achievements, or the small joys that bring a smile to your face. Allow yourself to feel the positive emotions associated with these thoughts. This exercise helps liberate you from the pursuit of fleeting happiness and fosters lasting fulfillment and appreciation for what you already have.

Regular gratitude visualization trains our minds to discover happiness in the present moment, encouraging resilience in the face of life's ups and downs. Also, it breaks the cycle of the hedonic treadmill, where we constantly chase external sources of happiness without finding lasting contentment.

You may have come across the phrase "fake it till you make it." In other words, it means to act like a happy person—smile, laugh, engage with others, and project energy and enthusiasm—even if you don't feel happy initially. Interestingly, this simulated behavior can actually lead to a happier state. Not only will people respond to you more positively, but you'll find yourself genuinely feeling happier through this practice.

In a nutshell: Long-term happiness and balance come from finding meaning and contentment in our daily experiences, not from chasing short-lived pleasures. We've learned how gratitude and positive thinking can boost happiness, and how achieving balance in life involves skillfully juggling all the things that matter to us without neglecting any.

Finding this equilibrium entails making time for work, family, self-care, and enjoyable activities to avoid feeling overwhelmed or drained. When you find that sweet spot, you'll experience greater happiness and contentment because you're attentively caring for all essential elements in a harmonious manner.

Now as we move into Step 3, our focus shifts toward making significant progress with our goals. Fulfillment is attained by aligning our actions with our values and passions. So, let's dive in and learn how to make our dreams come true while fostering a sense of happiness and balance throughout our journey. Let's continue on this incredible adventure together.

JOURNAL PROMPTS

- What can you add to your daily routine to include self-care as a priority?
- What can you do to free up time to connect with friends and family more often?
- What activities need to be on your planner that make you feel happy and fulfilled?
- List five things you're really grateful for and how can you prioritize them in your daily life.

RECOMMENDED RESOURCES
TO LEARN MORE ON THIS TOPIC

Book: *The Balance Equation* by Rob Fiance and Stuart Rosenblum

Video: *Three Rules for Better Work–Life Balance*

PART IV

STEP 3

Achieve Consistent *Progress*

18. PROGRESS

You are what you do, not what you say you do.
— CARL JUNG

Challenges are what make life interesting.
Overcoming them is what makes life meaningful.
— UNKNOWN

Progress (verb) – to move forward toward a destination.

Progress (noun) – growth or development; a movement toward a goal.

Obstacle – something that impedes progress or achievement.

Progress comes from taking action and overcoming obstacles. It means you need to stop talking about doing something and start acting on your plans. You can learn to do this, and my goal is to guide you in the process. Changing your approach is essential if your previous way of thinking, feeling, and acting hasn't led you to your desired destination. So, let's get started.

To understand how change occurs, we'll first discuss the

cycle of thoughts, feelings, and behavior. One useful concept is the *cognitive triangle*, commonly utilized in cognitive behavioral therapy. It suggests that our thoughts influence how we feel, which, in turn, impacts our actions, leading back to our thoughts, and so forth. To change our actions, we must first change the way we think.[30]

Our brains tend to get accustomed to the way we've always done things, making it challenging to disrupt this cycle. Consequently, changing our thoughts requires sustained and active effort over an extended period. In the following chapters, we will look at each side of the triangle and the skills you can learn and master to take charge of your thoughts and feelings, granting you the freedom to choose how you respond to situations and challenges. Importantly, you'll learn to handle obstacles by viewing them as opportunities for learning and personal growth.

By now, having read this far, you should have:

- a clear understanding of who you are, including your aptitudes, passions, and values;
- purposes that motivate you and drive you toward your goals;
- knowledge of your starting point on this journey of change;
- a vision of where you want to go and who you aspire to become; and
- a detailed plan, complete with specific goals and actionable steps to serve as your roadmap toward personal growth and fulfillment.

With this strong foundation, you are prepared to make progress on your transformative journey, guided by purpose, and you will become empowered to overcome any challenges

---

30 Aaron T. Beck, *Cognitive Therapy of Depression*, 1979.

that arise.

One crucial consideration to keep in mind is that once you take that step forward and begin your journey, you must hold yourself accountable and take ownership of the outcomes. No excuses, no blame—it's on you. By following the guidance I am about to provide, you will overcome the numerous hurdles you'll face and build the confidence to persevere.

As you begin to alter your thoughts within the cognitive triangle and take bolder actions, you will inevitably encounter adversity, leading to various levels of stress, disappointment, and uncertainty. Leaning into adversity, you'll encounter some formidable obstacles, but fear not, for you are about to learn how to effectively handle and overcome them.

Negative self-talk like "Why try when I'll probably fail?" often holds people back from even starting when they set a goal. Some may even give up at the first sign of an obstacle, validating their initial doubts with an "I told you so." Consequently, they quickly retreat to the safety of their comfort zone, unwilling to endure the physical or mental discomfort that arises from stretching beyond it, thus missing out on valuable opportunities for learning and growth.

I have compiled a list of common internal obstacles, rooted in our thoughts, that prevent people from taking the first step or lead them to quit when faced with challenges:

- Self-doubt: believing that the task is too difficult or that you're lacking the necessary time, money, or energy.
- Negative mindset: holding the belief that you'll never acquire all the knowledge needed for success.
- Incomplete commitment: a lack of dedication to a task, goal, or relationship.
- Unrealistic expectations: expecting instant results and giving up when things become challenging.
- Courage and resilience: without these traits, we succumb

to the first obstacle we encounter.

- Laziness: being unwilling to put in the necessary effort for self-improvement.
- Self-accountability: lacking a method to measure personal progress or results, or lacking a support system for motivation or reminders of your purpose.
- Procrastination: delaying action by convincing yourself it's not the right time or getting trapped in paralysis by analysis.
- Preparation: failing to plan how to tackle the numerous obstacles that will arise.
- Fear of failure: insufficient self-confidence or lacking the right mindset to face challenges.
- Immediate gratification: unable to forego short-term pleasures for the promise of a better future.

Recognizing and addressing these common obstacles is essential for fostering the determination and resilience needed to overcome adversity and achieve your goals. Many of us begin pursuing a goal with energy, motivation, and excitement. We focus on the reward and how cool it will feel to attain it. However, as we take those first steps, we come face-to-face with the realization of the significant effort required to achieve our objectives.

The good news is that all of the internal obstacles listed above are within your control to overcome. It's a matter of retraining your mind and committing to the hard work that lies ahead. These obstacles begin with your way of thinking about yourself and the world around you. Moreover, employing an effective strategy can also help you conquer external obstacles that originate from outside influences, such as peer pressure, job loss, growing up in poverty, prejudice, or limited educational opportunities.

A valuable strategy to avoid getting tripped up is to first prepare yourself for the challenges that you'll encounter while working toward your goal. Then, learn to shift your focus back to the ultimate reward and your "why" when the going gets tough. Remind yourself why this pursuit is essential, and let that serve as a guiding light to keep you moving forward.

Perhaps your career didn't develop as you had hoped, or your retirement savings aren't as substantial due to disappointing investments. Maybe some of your relationships fell apart due to a lack of effort, or you experienced health issues or childhood trauma. Accept them as part of your life, but then make a determined effort to not let these past issues prevent you from living a meaningful life now. Instead, view them as valuable learning experiences that contribute to your growth and personal development.

Sometimes it helps to consider every day a fresh start. Write down, "Beginning tomorrow I'm getting back on track." Acknowledge that today might not have been perfect, but tomorrow offers a new opportunity for progress.

In a nutshell: Don't be that person who is always preparing to start a journey but always seems to have a reason for not starting today. It's never easy, but it's time to let go of the past; you can't change it. Instead, focus on making today a successful day. Whether it's your limiting beliefs, procrastination, or fixed mindset, you have the power to change how you think about yourself and, as a result, how you act.

In the upcoming chapters, we will explore the essential knowledge, skills, and habits required to kickstart your journey and keep the energy going. As you improve in all these areas, you enhance your ability to overcome obstacles and confidently navigate from where you are today to where you want to go. It all begins with learning to think positively and believing in your capacity to achieve your goals.

JOURNAL PROMPTS

List all the positive changes you have already made in your life.

- What's holding you back from what you really want to do? Do you have a plan to acquire the resources you need to move forward?
- What is something you gave up on? Would you try it again? What would you do differently this time?
- Write down five things you can do now to prepare yourself to overcome obstacles.

RECOMMENDED RESOURCES TO LEARN MORE ON THIS TOPIC

Book: *The Obstacle Is the Way* by Ryan Holiday

Video: *Seven Secrets to Becoming Mentally Tougher* by Psych2Go

19. THOUGHTS AND BELIEFS

*You begin to fly when you let go of self-limiting beliefs and
allow your mind and aspirations to rise to greater heights.*
— BRIAN TRACY

*Whether you think you can or
you think you can't, you're right.*
— HENRY FORD

Thoughts – usually short-lived ideas, memories, and visions.

Beliefs – convictions that we generally accept to be true,
without actual evidence or proof.

Self-talk – your inner voice, combining thoughts and beliefs.

In the long run, your beliefs about yourself shape your reality.
Your mindset and attitude have a profound effect on how you
think, feel, and then behave in any given situation. What you
believe about yourself significantly influences your success or
failure. If you hold unwavering belief in your ability to succeed,
you're more likely to bring that vision to fruition. It's not just

about wishing or hoping; it's about believing in your potential and being willing to work hard to achieve your goals.

Thoughts are the language of the brain and feelings are the language of the body. This chapter will focus on thoughts and beliefs, which directly impact our feelings and emotions, which will be discussed in the next chapter. Feelings and emotions, in turn, influence our behaviors, which lie at the core of Step 3. For example, if you believe you understand the material for an upcoming quiz, you'll feel at ease and self-assured about your prospects, allowing you to have a restful night's sleep beforehand. Consequently, you increase your likelihood of performing exceptionally well and achieving a high score on the quiz.

If you believe in yourself, possess the desire to succeed, and maintain a positive attitude and an open mindset, the path forward will become evident. Naturally, you'll encounter mistakes along the way, but with perseverance, you will ultimately achieve success. By rejecting excuses and overcoming the fear of failure, you'll undergo growth, build confidence, and enhance your effectiveness. Age, health, and events from your past do not serves as barriers; positive thinking benefits us all.

I have learned about two types of mindsets known as fixed and growth. A fixed (or 'limited') mindset is the belief that there are inherent limitations to what you can achieve in your life. In contrast, a growth (or 'open') mindset is the belief that you can enhance your abilities through dedication and hard work.[31]

Your mindset markedly influences how you think, feel, and behave in any given situation. Our beliefs often originate from our experiences, or from accepting what others tell us to be true. Many of our core beliefs take shape during childhood. We turn these experiences or words into stories we tell ourselves, eventually forming our reality.

However, these self-beliefs are not always accurate, healthy,

---

31 Carol Dweck, *Mindset*, 2019.

or helpful. They can influence our interpretation of events and impact the actions we take, potentially limiting our opportunities and impeding our ability to reach our goals or accomplish great things.

With a fixed attitude or belief, we risk remaining perpetually stuck without growth or development. In contrast, individuals with a growth mindset, who believe in their potential for improvement, tend to experience more success in life than those with a fixed mindset.

I was once told by my junior high art teacher, "You will never be good at art". I believed her and subsequently avoided taking any art classes through the end of high school. But was she right? I wonder if having a different, more encouraging teacher could have led me to believe more positively in my ability to create art.

Focusing on the reasons you are likely to succeed rather than on the reasons you're likely to fail yields several positive benefits for your mindset and actions. You become more solution-oriented and willing to learn from mistakes. You become proactive in seeking opportunities for growth and improvement instead of being paralyzed by fear of failure.

To make this shift, start by challenging any negative thoughts about yourself. Replace them with positive affirmations and surround yourself with supportive people. Set achievable goals and celebrate your progress, no matter how small. Remember, success often comes with challenges, but maintaining a positive outlook on your potential for success will help you overcome them with determination. With this mindset, you'll unlock your full potential and achieve greater things in life.

Consider some potential limiting beliefs that many people have: "it's too hard," "I'm not smart enough," "I don't have the time," or "I can't afford it." We have all likely experienced these beliefs at some point in our lives, and they often lead to negative emotions such as self-pity or fear of failure, ultimately preventing us from even trying.

Negative thinking, or self-talk, is often derived from past failures, regrets, or disappointments. For example, not getting a desired promotion can trigger negative thoughts. To counteract these negative patterns, it's essential to talk to yourself with a positive voice and challenge those thoughts. When negative thoughts arise, mindfully identify them, question their source and truthfulness, and if found to be unfounded, replace them with more realistic and positive affirmations instead of avoiding or denying them.

Paying attention to negative thoughts and adopting positive self-talk can greatly impact how you perceive yourself. By telling yourself "I have the time, intelligence, skill, and resources to do this" and genuinely believing in this truth, you will begin to feel and act accordingly, empowering yourself to take on challenges and achieve your goals.

You can transition from a fixed mindset to a growth mindset by focusing on the following strategies:

- Dedicate more time to activities that bring you joy, optimism, and energy.
- Reduce the time spent on draining activities that leave you feeling depleted.
- Engage in consistent positive and constructive self-talk.
- Accept challenges and step out of your comfort zone, even if it feels intimidating.
- Prioritize your physical, mental, and financial health.
- Surround yourself with positive individuals who inspire and motivate you.
- Maintain a thirst for knowledge by reading books, listening to podcasts, and watching videos about positive thinking and an open mindset.
- Take ownership of your decisions and your actions; avoid blaming others.

- Eliminate negative language from your vocabulary, such as using words like *can't*, *nothing*, or *never*.

Choose to tell yourself a different story. The power lies in the narrative we create within ourselves. Instead of saying you can't do something, tell yourself that you can learn anything. Overcome the fear of failure, whether from past experiences or future possibilities. While fear is natural, acknowledge it when it arises and choose to act in spite of it. Welcome it as a teacher, showing you that your original belief was limiting and untrue, and that you possess untapped capabilities. Managing fear removes barriers to acquiring a growth mindset.

Important research highlights the significance of how we interpret feelings like fear. Fear consists of two components: the physical changes in our body, such as increased heart rate, rapid breathing, tense muscles, and sweating, and then our interpretation of these changes. We have control over the second aspect. Rather than saying, "I'm frightened," we can reframe it positively by telling ourselves, "My body is preparing me to face a challenge with extra resources." By altering our interpretation, we can embrace fear as a source of strength to conquer challenges and approach them confidently.[32]

Pay attention to any negative self-talk and feelings. Your old, repressed thoughts and traumatic memories never totally go away. You need to realize they are only thoughts that you can learn to ignore and let pass. This gives you power to change your self-talk and your response to it.

Your thoughts play a crucial role in either moving you forward or holding you back. When you overthink, you can feel overwhelmed, leading to inaction. Negative thoughts can impede your creativity and progress. However, you have the power to control your thoughts, so why not choose new

32 Martin E.P. Seligman, *Authentic Happiness*, 2007.

positive ones to move you in the right direction?

To choose new thoughts, you first need to recognize when you find yourself overthinking or dwelling on negative thoughts. When you catch yourself in this pattern, pause and take a deep breath. Then, challenge those negative thoughts and replace them with more constructive ones. For example, if you catch yourself thinking, "I can't do this, it's too difficult," reframe it into something like, "This may be challenging, but I am capable of learning and growing through the process."

Practicing mindfulness can also help you become more aware of your thoughts and emotions. Engaging in regular physical activity and spending time in nature can also help to clear your mind and improve your overall wellbeing.

You are the one preventing yourself from living your dream. Having a growth mindset will help you overcome your self-limiting beliefs, destructive emotions, and harmful habits. Don't let a limited mindset stop you from reaching your goals and living a meaningful life. Change your self-image and you will change your life.

Remember that it takes time and effort to change thought patterns, so be patient with yourself. Be kind and compassionate, just as you would be with a friend. Over time, with consistent practice, you'll notice that you can control your thoughts more effectively, allowing you to move forward with confidence and positivity, and achieve your goals with greater ease.

In a nutshell: In this chapter, we've explored the incredible power of our thoughts and beliefs in shaping our reality. By adopting an open and growth-oriented mindset, we conquer self-limiting beliefs and fear. Changing our thought patterns allows us to unlock our full potential and create a deeply fulfilling life.

If you find it challenging to push past negative thoughts and self-talk with your own willpower, I recommend seeking the assistance of a licensed therapist. It's important to find a solution before it evolves into a difficult outcome, such as losing your job or a good friend. Understanding the origin of your thoughts will help you identify the cause and find effective solutions to manage them.

As we move forward, the next chapter will shed light on the profound connection between our thoughts and our emotions.

JOURNAL PROMPTS

- What steps can you take to practice more positive self-talk?
- What benefits has your positive mindset brought you so far?
- What are some limiting beliefs that might be holding you back and how can you change them?
- Note your positive and negative thoughts for the next few hours. How many are there of each? Do they tend to repeat?

RECOMMENDED RESOURCES TO LEARN MORE ON THIS TOPIC

Book: *365 Days of Positive Self-Talk* by Shad Helmstetter

Book: *Mind Your Mindset* by Michael Hyatt and Megan Hyatt Miller

Video: *A Simple Trick to Improve Positive Thinking* by Alison Ledgerwood

20. FEELINGS AND EMOTIONS

You own your feelings.
You own your thoughts. You control both.
— CARLOS WALLACE

It is a choice. No matter how frustrating or boring or constraining or painful or oppressive our experience, we can always choose how we respond.
— EDITH EGAR

Emotions – a mental state that originates as sensations in the body.

Feelings – influenced by our emotions but are generated from our mental thoughts.

There is a long list of negative emotions that can have detrimental effects on self-esteem, self-confidence, and overall happiness with life. While these emotions are often viewed as something to be avoided or ignored, experiencing them can be a healthy part of life. However, if left unmanaged, they can interfere with your ability to achieve your goals and lead a fulfilling life.

Negative emotions can arise as a single, short-term reaction to a difficult event, such as a missed opportunity, or they may be recurring if they originate from underlying issues like unmet needs, relationship problems, or poor coping skills. These emotions can serve as signals, indicating that there may be underlying problems that need resolution, even if everything appears fine on the surface. Paying attention to these signals provides valuable insights for making positive changes in our lives.

Ignoring these emotions prevents you from making necessary changes and can lead to continued negative feelings. Some common types of negative emotions that hold us back from making progress are anger, anxiety, fear, jealousy, shame, sadness, and regret. Each of these emotions can constrain our growth.

In this chapter, we will focus on *regret* as an example to demonstrate how negative emotions must be acknowledged and addressed, allowing us to move forward with our plans in life. While an entire chapter could be written on the causes for each of these emotions, our primary aim is to understand the significance of dealing with them effectively. Regret may emerge from wishing we could undo a previous choice, contemplating missed opportunities, or recognizing unintended negative consequences resulting from our actions.

Anytime you make a choice or a decision, there is the possibility of feeling regret. It's an unavoidable consequence of living life. Most people have thoughts about the life they should have had instead of the one they currently live: "If only this had happened"; "If only that hadn't happened"; "I wish I had..."; "I wish I hadn't..."; "I never would have ended up here." These are the kinds of stories we tell ourselves.

We spend a significant amount of time wishing our lives were different, comparing ourselves to other people, and different versions of ourselves, forgetting that most lives contain degrees of good and bad. All of us have memories of countless mistakes and regrettable choices, but we can do little about them now except to better understand what happened, learn from them, and move forward.

Late in life, two common regrets reported by the elderly are not having had the courage to live a life true to themselves, and never pursuing their dreams. Fortunately, if you follow through on what you are learning in *Rise Above the Rut*, you can avoid nearing the end of your life with these same regrets.

Regrets have the power to make you to feel bad about yourself and trap you in a cycle of low self-esteem, diminishing your confidence for the future. This makes it difficult for you to move forward and try new things.

I could have spent my life in regret if I had continued with the routine work of a pharmacist, knowing that it was not a good fit for my interests, abilities, and values. I might have stayed stuck in that rut, accepting my fate without question. However, I refused to let that happen. Instead, I acknowledged my mistake and started envisioning a more meaningful career that aligned with my passions. I created a plan to make a career adjustment, setting and achieving the goal of getting an MBA, which led to a new career in pharmacy management.

As a result of pursuing my vision, my days at work became more meaningful, and I moved beyond the feelings of regret. Many years later, I unearthed a new purpose for my life, leading me down a path to becoming a writer, author, and independent publisher.

If you're experiencing regret about your chosen career, it's important to remember that it's never too late to make a change. Acknowledge that it might have been the wrong choice and develop a plan to explore a new career path that better suits your life vision. It may not be easy, but it will undoubtably be worth it in the end.

You can't go back and undo choices from the past that you now regret. However, you can be mindful and reflect on those decisions. Consider what you might have done differently and use this as a learning experience. Remember, your past doesn't have to dictate your future. Forgive yourself, and allow personal growth to take place. Use it as valuable information to guide you moving forward, becoming a wiser version of yourself.

The wiser you will focus on what's within your control, including your attitude and effort. Concentrate on what you can do to address a problem or overcome an obstacle, rather than dwelling on what you cannot change. Continually tell yourself that you feel great, and you'll start to experience the positive effects. Build up more positive self-talk, and you'll notice a positive shift in how you feel both mentally and physically.

Author Joyce Chapman claims that "more than anything, our attitude in approaching a task will determine our success or failure."[33] For instance:

- Negative attitude: "Every time I have tried losing weight in the past I have failed. I doubt that this time will be any different." This is acting pessimistic.
- Positive attitude: "I expect to look and feel great now that I am going to lose twenty pounds." This is acting optimistic.

Which of these attitudes is more likely to lead to success?

In a nutshell: The wisdom of elders serves as a reminder that regrets often originate from actions not taken rather than from actions taken—even if they didn't work out. Negative emotions should not serve as an excuse to hold you back from pursuing potentially meaningful and rewarding endeavors. Identify and welcome your emotions, including fear and regret, and then move forward with renewed purpose in life, regardless of your age.

---

33 Joyce Chapman, *Live Your Dream*, 2002.

If these feelings persist and start to interfere with your ability to live your life normally, it's important to seek professional help. A mental health professional can help you identify the underlying causes of your feelings and develop a treatment plan that works for you.

Our thoughts, feelings, and behavior are interconnected, each influencing the other. In the next chapter we will look at the behavior side of the cognitive triangle, including habit creation.

JOURNAL PROMPTS

- What negative emotions have you experienced today? What were the thoughts that led to these emotions?
- What childhood memories impact your adult life? How does holding onto negative emotions impact your everyday life?
- What would you love to do that the fear of failure is stopping you from doing?

RECOMMENDED RESOURCES TO LEARN MORE ON THIS TOPIC

Book: *Master Your Emotions* by Thibaut Meurisse

Book: *Stop Overthinking* by Nick Trenton

Video: *How to Manage Your Emotions* by Daniel Stankler

21. BEHAVIOR AND HABITS

Your life today is essentially the sum of your habits.
— JAMES CLEAR

*Our daily decisions and habits have a huge
impact on both our levels of happiness and success.*
— SHAWN ANCHOR

Behavior – the way in which one acts in response to internal or external stimuli.

Habit – a behavioral pattern that we repeat often.

Habit loop – a repetitive cycle involving a trigger or cue, followed by an action, and then a reward.

Our behavior acts like a window for viewing our true selves, displaying our self-image, values, and beliefs. Behavior is the third side of the cognitive triangle. The first two sides, thoughts and feelings, were discussed in the previous two chapters. Actions, as they say, speak louder than words, offering valuable insights into our inner world.

There are two types of behavior discussed in the literature. First, innate behavior is genetically hardwired and manifests without any prior experience or training. Examples include seeking out food when hungry or exhibiting the fight-or-flight response when our survival is threatened.

Second, learned behavior does not come naturally. It develops through experience or training. Examples range from driving a car to using a cell phone. Much of our learned behavior becomes habitual. In this chapter, we will focus on learned behavior, examining how unhelpful behavior can keep us stuck and suffocate our growth and goal achievement.

Feelings or emotions can significantly influence our actions. For instance, feeling happy may lead us to do kind deeds. While anger might prompt us to act mean. Habits are behaviors that become embedded from repetition. They develop their own momentum, driven by the pleasure they provide or as a response to stress and anxiety, eventually becoming automatic actions.

Habits are formed through a loop consisting of a trigger, behavior, and reward. For example, hunger acts as the trigger, followed by the behavior of eating a meal or a snack, leading to the reward of feeling full or satisfied, thus completing the habit loop.

Throughout our daily lives, we engage in a series of habits that shape our routines and responses, supporting us in both favorable and challenging times. Our habits define our identity, as we are what we consistently do. They should reflect our purpose, values, and priorities, just like flossing and brushing our teeth twice a day, if we value good oral health.

Unfortunately, we can also develop unhelpful habits that bring negative consequences. Your plans and goals should include replacing habits that create roadblocks to achieving these goals with habits that are useful in making progress. Examples of unhelpful habits that constrain growth and progress include:

- consistently being late;
- engaging in negative self-talk or being hard on yourself;
- struggling to control your emotions effectively;
- failing to defer gratification and give in to immediate desires;
- self-sabotaging your own efforts;
- mindlessly snacking on junk food;
- procrastinating or leaving tasks for the last minute;
- continuously postponing your goals;
- attempting to multi-task or taking on too much at once;
- blaming others for your lack of success;
- avoiding problems rather than facing them head-on;
- constant complaining and dwelling on grievances;
- striving for perfectionism, leading to unnecessary stress;
- trying to control every aspect of your life and not allowing room for flexibility;
- spending excessive time planning and insufficient time taking action;
- living too much in the past or worrying too much about the future;
- giving up quickly or refusing to learn anything new;
- remaining in unhealthy relationships that hold you back;
- living in a life filled with constant crises rather than seeking stability;
- settling for a mediocre life instead of striving for excellence;
- engaging in habits such as smoking or neglecting regular exercise.

By identifying and addressing these unhelpful habits, you make it easier to pave the way for personal growth and advance toward your goals.

Starting or changing a habit can be difficult. Have you ever attempted to establish a routine of going to a fitness center regularly? It's all too tempting to hit the snooze button and opt for extra sleep, instead of getting up early to exercise. When we lack focus on our long-term goals and purpose, we tend to prioritize immediate gratification, such as going back to sleep, over the benefits of exercising.

This inclination to value smaller, instant rewards, over larger, future rewards is known as "present bias.[34]" Given how habits significantly impact our ability to succeed, I'll put on my behavioral health pharmacist hat for a moment and review a bit of neuroscience, but I'll be brief. Understanding a little of how habits form in the brain helps clarify why altering them requires conscious effort.

As you repeat an activity, your brain will start connecting lots of neurons. Over time, your brain seeks efficiency and conserves energy by developing the most efficient or shortest pathway. The pathway can take three to six months to fully form, and once it does, the habit becomes automatic. Performing the activity as a habit requires less energy than when you had to consciously think about it and motivate yourself.[35]

Keep in mind that these neuron pathways are not permanent. If you stop repeating the process, the habit pathway will start to dismantle, which usually happens within a few days to a few weeks. Newer habit pathways tend to dismantle more quickly, as your brain tries to conserve the energy by eliminating unused pathways.

To retain a habit, you must continue the activity. We have probably all heard the expression "Use it or lose it, " which applies to neural pathways as well. Habits save time and

---

34 Katy Milkman, *How to Change*, 2021.

35 Azzy Aslam, "Changing Habits - Changing Lives," 2022.

energy, as they eliminate the need to stop and think about what to do or whether you want to do it. Automatic habits encompass activities like brushing your teeth before bed or making your morning coffee.

At some point, you'll come to the realization that certain habits are harming you. Whether it's the weight you gained, the money you spent on cigarettes, or the health consequences of added stress or anxiety, these negative feelings prompt you consider changing your unhelpful habits.

Long-term change or creating new habits is more challenging than short-term changes. Consider the difference between eating healthy for one day compared to sustaining it every day for the rest of your life. How can you increase the likelihood of a changed habit becoming a long-term change, rather than fizzling out after a few weeks or months? Here are some suggestions:

- The habit change has to be something you earnestly want to do. Choose habit replacements that are aligned with your mission and goals. Know why you are doing this.
- Only focus on one habit change at a time. Instead of just trying to quit an unhelpful habit, replace it with a helpful habit.
- It's best to start with small steps and increase slowly but regularly. Moderate, incremental change that is sustainable is the best way to change or create a continuing helpful habit. Want to exercise? Start with just five to ten minutes each day.
- Write down your plan to change a habit, including how it will benefit you. Set a goal to specify the what, when, and where of the trigger or cue, your new response to it, and your reward for success. Track your habit progress in your daily planner.

- It helps to remember the first step of the habit loop: cues. Establish a new visible cue to remind you of the habit you are trying to learn—like some floss taped to your bathroom mirror, or your journal with a pen sitting on your bedside table.
- Set up a positive reinforcement or reward for responding correctly to the cue. Connect that first great cup of coffee to your journaling instead of drinking it while scrolling on your phone; or listen to a podcast you enjoy only while doing your workout.
- Practice mindfulness: focus on reminding yourself why you are doing this. Be aware of any urge to procrastinate or talk yourself out of it. Visualize how your life will be improved having successfully changed the habit.
- Consider, and then write down, all your obstacles to change and the corresponding solutions to overcome each one. For instance, have apples in your house instead of donuts.
- Keep yourself accountable and ask a support person to check in on you.
- Typically, urges to engage in unhelpful habits last for about a minute or two. Try deep breathing, drinking a glass of water, or taking a walk, to help them pass. Then, reward yourself.
- Don't make any exceptions. Whenever a cue arises, ensure you perform the new helpful action. If you happen to falter, take the time to review and learn from your mistake, and then renew your commitment.

In a nutshell: Behavior, including habits, is the third side of the cognitive triangle. A habit is a learned sequence of actions repeated on a regular basis. Some habits are useful, while others can be harmful actions or inactions. Habits can form unintentionally, or they can be intentionally shaped or eliminated to suit our personal goals.

We all have unhelpful habits we would like to change or improve upon. Understanding how habits are formed allows us to break the habit loop and train our brain to stop self-sabotaging our growth and progress. Unhelpful habits keep you unhappy, stuck, and acting in ways that don't align with your true self. Alternatively, healthy behavior and habits are in line with your values and goals.

To achieve your goals, it requires acquiring knowledge and developing skills to overcome the discomfort that arises from venturing into new territory and pushing beyond your comfort zone. These skills include commitment, proactivity, resilience, and more. In the next few chapters, you will gain additional knowledge and tools needed to confidently advance toward your vision.

JOURNAL PROMPTS

- List three habits you would like to add or change, write down why they are important, and design a specific plan to make each happen. How will achieving each one make you feel and how will your life improve? Consider habits for healthier eating, routine exercising, saving money, and reducing stress in your life.
- How can you act more in alignment with your core beliefs?

RECOMMENDED RESOURCES TO LEARN MORE ON THIS TOPIC

Book: *Atomic Habits* by James Clear

Book: *The Power of Habit* by Charles Duhigg

Podcast: *The Habit Coach* with Ashwind Doctor

Video: *How Habits Can Change Your Life (and Your Brain)* by Be Smart

22. PACK A TOOLKIT FOR YOUR JOURNEY

Enjoy the journey and try to get better every day.
And don't lose the passion and love for what you do.
— NADIA COMANECI

My career is a journey for me, and any journey
is incomplete without the struggle.
— YAMI GAUTAM

Journey – passage or progress from one location or condition to another.

Tool – a device used to carry out a particular function.

Skill – a learned ability, through practice, to do an activity or job well.

I hope you're filled with excitement as you set sail toward your visions and goals. However, before you venture too far into the uncharted waters of your dreams, let's assemble a toolkit equipped with the skills, knowledge, and habits needed to make steady progress toward your destination. While no journey is without challenges, you'll be well-prepared to overcome any obstacles and position yourself for success.

We'll explore various tools that you need, and the best part is that all these tools can be learned, improved, and even mastered. In addition to the fundamental tools, bring along personal qualities such as intention, desire, courage, resilience, growth mindset, positive attitude, and self-confidence. Just like competent captains ensure they have the necessary supplies before setting sail, these tools and qualities will equip you to navigate through any challenges that come your way.

To make good progress and achieve your goals, you will need to welcome the pain, discomfort, and frustration that come with taking any risk and expanding your comfort zone. You need to do what you've never done before. That is how you learn and grow. Understand how to use your tools and make them part of who you are.

Progress is a journey that starts with small steps and grows with each passing day. The more you believe in yourself and perform well every day, the more success you will achieve.

I want you to feel confident in your ability to overcome every challenge and obstacle that comes your way. We will always encounter headwinds in life, but most resistance comes from our own thoughts and feelings. Every obstacle can be overcome. Whether the source is external or internal, we must be ready to persevere. By enhancing your knowledge, skills, and habits, the following positive shifts will occur:

- You'll become able to practice positive self-talk.
- You'll be encouraging and supportive to yourself.
- You'll view failures as opportunities to improve. You'll learn from them and move on.
- You'll find ways to enjoy what you are doing. Take a moment to celebrate your accomplishments.

- You'll do what makes you happy. Don't let others dictate your life.
- You'll expand your horizons as you push yourself outside of your comfort zone. Get comfortable with being uncomfortable.
- You'll eliminate or block out unhelpful distractions and improve your focus and concentration.
- You'll grow as a person and become the best version of yourself.

Before you start learning more about these tools and begin crafting them, it's important to understand that some personal qualities can help you take control and reach your goals, while others can hamper you. The helpful ones mobilize you into action that is beneficial and productive. As we talked about in Chapter 20: Feelings and Emotions, fear can be helpful, but regret will slow you down. Make fear your friend. You're stronger than you think. Taking purposeful action opens up a clearer path that helps you manage and overcome your fear.

Almost everyone I speak with about fear says they have experienced a persistent internalized fear of being exposed as a fraud. It is so common it has a name, the *Imposter identity syndrome*.[36] It is a psychological phenomenon that makes you feel like you are not as competent as others think you are.

We all experience fear. Don't let it rob you of opportunities or experiences you want to have in your life. You can't ignore fear, but you can learn to deal with it. I suggest using the five-second countdown rule and then reframing your thoughts to why you should be excited about what you are doing. When opportunity arises, and fear starts to creep in, count 5-4-3-2-1 and focus on what it will look like and how you will feel when you do it successfully. This allows you to maintain control over

---

36 Katty Kay, Claire Shipman, *The Confidence Code*, 2018.

what you are thinking, feeling, and how you behave. Choose to change your life in just five seconds.[37]

Some personal qualities that help you overcome fear include learning to trust yourself and your decisions, taking ownership of your life and purposefully acting, identifying fear components like rejection or failure and neutralizing them, and building self-esteem.

In a nutshell: To overcome challenges and achieve success, you need three important components: skills, knowledge, and habits. These three elements work together like a team to help you figure things out and keep you moving toward your goals.

Don't let tough circumstances or a difficult past define you. You have the power to shape your own path and create the life you desire by learning to understand and use the three components. So, in the next chapter we will explore the power of continuous learning.

---

37 Mel Robbins, *The 5 Second Rule*, 2017.

JOURNAL PROMPTS

- What would it mean for you to go forward without regretting the past? Think about your regrets and decide whether you really need to carry them into tomorrow.
- When you look at life, do you typically notice only the bad things that happen, or do you also notice the many wonderful events that take place daily and the potential opportunities? Why do you think this is so? How does this affect your approach to overcoming life's challenges?
- Do you feel confident about your direction? Or does your mind tend to wander aimlessly at times? What changes could you make in your thinking to align with your vision?

RECOMMENDED RESOURCES TO LEARN MORE ON THIS TOPIC

Book: *Get Out of Your Own Way* by Mark Goulston and Philip Goldberg

Book: *The Mountain Is You* by Brianna Wiest

Video: *Preparation Is the Key to Overcoming Obstacles* by Jim Rohn

23. LEARNING

*An investment in knowledge always
pays the best interest.*
— BENJAMIN FRANKLIN

*The great aim of education is
not knowledge but action.*
— HERBERT SPENCER

Learning – the acquisition of knowledge, skills, and qualities through experience, study, or by being taught.

Knowledge – the understanding of a subject that you get from experience or study.

Welcome to the area of learning, a skill that sets us free in life. As we journey forward and encounter obstacles, remember that having confidence in our ability to handle whatever comes our way is key. It's also important to recognize that we'll need to keep learning and practicing to become the person we aspire to be. As we learn and practice new skills, we continuously grow and become more competent.

Learn. Grow. Thrive. I recently saw this written on the side of a school bus while visiting St. Petersburg, Florida. Learning is something we do every day. It is an important part of personal development, and it helps you understand the world around you.

Learning isn't confined to the classroom. We learn as we encounter new information, pay attention to it, coordinate it with what we already know, store it in our memory, and then apply it to overcome future obstacles and improve our lives.

It's natural to feel frustrated when you first start learning something new. You have no idea what you are doing or what to focus on. So, it's important to understand that if you remain confident and push past these early struggles, you will successfully improve your competence. If you have tried to learn a new language, you have likely experienced this initial frustration.

The process of learning can start by looking up the meaning of a word in the dictionary or watching a video on fixing a jammed disposal. Both instances involve learning from the exposure to new information. Your learning and skills continue to develop as you use the word in a conversation, or successfully unjam the disposal.

The learning process enables us to acquire various useful life skills, such as:

- time management, mindfulness, and journaling (which we have already discussed);
- communication and interpersonal issues;
- financial management;
- critical thinking;
- professional and business skills;
- resilience; and
- many more.

In Chapter twenty-one, we learned how habits work, involving a cue, action, and reward. Now let's see how learning new skills can create a similar habit loop for positive change. Imagine you want to build a successful business. By putting effort into learning and improving key skills, you'll see yourself getting better. This progress boosts your confidence in reaching your goal. It changes how you act, making you feel more like a successful business owner. This shift becomes a habit loop, where your actions become a routine, driven by the reward of growth. This cycle keeps you motivated to keep learning and improving.

By actively pursuing short-term goals, such as reading a book about business planning or attending an online business accounting course, you not only improve your ability to operate a successful business, but also cultivate a mindset of continuous learning that will benefit you throughout your entrepreneurial journey.

As you witness the positive impact of learning on your business growth, it becomes evident that this process of skill development isn't confined to entrepreneurship alone. Just as you've honed your abilities to navigate the business landscape, the practice of learning and improvement will prove essential in mastering a diverse range of valuable skills.

To make learning an integral and intentional part of your routine, ensure that these activities are incorporated into your plan, complete with goals to keep yourself on track. Integrate your learning journey into your daily planner by outlining the necessary steps for enhancing your competence. Furthermore, remember to persistently engage in mindfulness, visualization, and journaling practices, to foster ongoing and sustainable growth.

If you're up for exciting experiences, why not explore new hobbies or interests that truly spark joy? You can dive into painting, photography, music, computer programming, or even learn more about the latest app on your phone. The best part is that learning and practicing will be a breeze and loads of fun, when you're naturally inclined toward it.

Discover meaningful activities that provide focused and sustained learning opportunities, to enhance your skills. Consider watching someone who is already skilled, joining clubs or groups with training options, attending insightful conferences or seminars, or enrolling in courses at your local college. There's a wealth of possibilities for your personal growth and development.

Keep in mind that improving a skill or ability takes desire, time, and resilience. It doesn't need to happen quickly, but consistently putting in effort will lead to lifelong benefits. In fact, scientific research has shown that learning can reduce the intellectual impacts of aging.[38] While your body may face limitations, a nourished brain can invigorate life at any age.

Thinking creatively can boost your motivation. Ask yourself how you can learn new and improved ways to achieve better results. Every morning, before starting your day, ask yourself, "How can I excel today?" Challenge your mind and broaden your horizons.

If you haven't yet uncovered your purpose, or set plans and goals to live your vision, you may lack motivation to learn. Having a clear vision of your future is essential to stay motivated for learning and growth.

In a nutshell: In this chapter, we've explored the immense benefits of continuous learning and practicing vital life skills. By broadening your knowledge and refining your abilities, you'll acquire the necessary tools to overcome obstacles, handle daily responsibilities, and seize promising opportunities when they emerge.

In addition, it's important to be mindful of how habits influence our behavior, as they can either propel us toward success or hinder our growth. In the next chapter, we will

---

38 Harvard Health Blog, "Back to school: Learning a new skill can slow cognitive aging," 2016.

examine additional proficiencies to bring along on your journey. These include the essential elements of desire, motivation, and commitment.

JOURNAL PROMPTS

- Write down five skills you would like to improve that could help you reach your goals. For each one, write down five sources for gaining the necessary information and experience. These could include books, videos, podcasts, classes, joining a club, or finding a mentor.
- Has a book, movie, television show, song, or video game ever inspired you to learn something new?
- When you have failed, what did you learn from it?
- What can you learn to improve your work performance?

RECOMMENDED RESOURCES TO LEARN MORE ON THIS TOPIC

Book: *How to Be Better at Almost Everything* by Pat Flynn

Video: *Five Tips to Improve Your Critical Thinking* by Samantha Agoos

24. DESIRE, MOTIVATION, AND COMMITMENT

Many people die with their music still in them. Why is this so?
Too often it is because they are always getting ready to live.
Before they know it, time runs out.
— OLIVER WENDALL HOLMES

Freedom is not the absence of commitment, but the ability
to choose—and commit myself to—what is best for me.
— PAULO COELHO

Desire – a strong feeling of wanting to have something or wishing for something to happen.

Motivation – the reason for acting or behaving in a particular way.

Commitment – a pledge to use your time and energy for something you believe in.

Desire is the spark that ignites the fire within us, motivating us to take that crucial first step on our journey. It serves as a compelling force driving us to take action. Without it, we wouldn't even bother assembling the necessary tools to progress along our path. We'd settle for a life with little ambition, rarely using our freedom to take charge and change our story. As a result, we'd sabotage any thought of commitment.

Without desire, our incentive to act diminishes, causing progress to grind to a halt and leaving us feeling trapped. If we lack desire for a short period of time, we may become bored, and if it's absent for an extended duration, a sense of depression can take hold.

But fear not! It's desire that moves us forward, giving our life direction and meaning. Your reading this book indicates that you have the desire to pursue something more significant in your life, and this very desire motivates you to keep reading, learning and growing. Follow this desire, for it holds the key to unlocking your full potential. You'll know you've got it right when you feel eager to take steps toward achieving your goals.

If at any point your desire starts to wane and procrastination creeps in, revisit your purpose and visualize how achieving your goals will enhance your life. Also, assess whether the tasks on your planner feel too big and overwhelming. If so, consider breaking them into smaller steps for now.

Sometimes, you'll come across signs that encourage you to make changes in your life. It could be feeling unenthusiastic about getting out of bed each morning, finding yourself calling off work more often, or noticing weight gain that leaves you dissatisfied with your appearance and wellbeing. These signals might be the beginning of the motivation you need to enhance your life. Once you begin your journey of self-improvement, motivation will enable you to overcome procrastination and other obstacles, providing the energy to keep moving forward.

Other signs that can motivate you to make changes in your life include the following:

- You think and dream about having a better life but have not actually done anything to make it happen.
- You feel stuck in a bad situation and feel jealous of others that are doing better.
- You are feeling anxious, depressed, or tired on most days.
- You are constantly worrying about what happened in the past and all the things that can go wrong in the future.

Life is too short to let it pass by without realizing your full potential. When you recognize these harmful behaviors and signs, it's a clear indication that it's time to shift how you handle your thoughts and emotions. Recognizing these signs is an opportunity to begin a journey of positive change. Here are some effective ways you can initiate that change:

- Practice acceptance rather than trying to avoid or deny negative thoughts. Then replace them with more positive, helpful ones.
- Review your personal purpose statement. Ensure that your daily activities align with your passions, values, and abilities.
- Learn to cope with feedback and criticism. Take a break from social media.
- Express negative emotions in a healthy way.
- Create opportunities for positivity in your life.
- Challenge your limiting beliefs.
- Be grateful more often.
- Cultivate an open mindset and positive attitude. Both are crucial for improving the way you think, feel, and act.

There are two primary types of motivation: intrinsic and extrinsic. Intrinsically motivated individuals are those who find genuine joy and fulfillment in the process of learning, growing, and accomplishing something meaningful that benefits not just themselves, but others as well. When they pursue goals that resonate with their sense of purpose, they feel a deep sense of satisfaction and drive.[39]

On the other hand, extrinsically motivated individuals prioritize external rewards, like money, fame, or recognition. While these external incentives might initially boost motivation, they often diminish over time, posing challenges to maintaining long-term commitment.

Understanding the distinction between intrinsic and extrinsic motivation can empower us to grow our commitment in a way that feels more natural and fulfilling. By nurturing our intrinsic motivation and seeking purpose-driven goals, we can clear the way for sustained and meaningful commitment, propelling us on a path toward growth and fulfillment.

When you commit, you promise or dedicate yourself to take specific action. You promise to do something and then follow through by doing it, without any excuses. When you fulfill a commitment, it builds self-trust and earns the trust of others.

Commitment is the dedication to getting something done, even in the face of foreseen and unforeseen hurdles. It requires you to move outside your comfort zone and do whatever is necessary to attain success. Even if you fail, it is an opportunity to learn, grow, and commit to a different action.

Individuals with commitment issues may experience mental distress and emotional difficulty when faced with situations that require dedication to a particular long-term goal. Commitment issues might affect one's performance at school or in the workplace, as well as one's romantic relationships. These

---

39 Daniel H. Pink, *Drive*, 2011.

challenges can hamper a person's progress in enhancing their quality of life. If you find that these difficulties persist and affect your daily functioning or well-being, it might indicate that professional therapy is a suitable option to explore.

Being committed is not always easy and calls for substantial mental resilience, especially in the face of adversity. Without making a sincere commitment, acting on our desires alone won't lead to significant achievements; we'll likely encounter mental and physical obstacles that we must overcome. Ultimately, a lack of commitment raises the likelihood of giving up when faced with challenges.

Dedicate yourself to having a positive attitude and promise to do whatever it takes. Also, strive for excellence in all you do, but avoid feeling like progress needs to be perfect. Avoid burnout from doing too much too soon or for too long. Remember that starting with small steps leads to big changes.

Fully commit to investing in yourself and your future. For instance, consider enrolling in a weekly evening class, such as one focused on STEM subjects, that can improve your thinking skills and expand your mental horizons. These classes can be idea starters that lead you toward a new career path. Improving your critical thinking ability can sometimes benefit you more than a college degree, as numerous accomplished small business owners have convincingly demonstrated.

According to Leon Ho, the founder and CEO of Lifehack, a major component of success is commitment.

A few ideas on how to keep commitments you make to yourself:

- Remind yourself of your purpose and plans and why you committed to doing this.
- Believe you can get this done.
- Have SMART goals: specific, measurable, achievable, relevant, and timebound.

- Write the individual steps on your daily calendar.
- Hold yourself accountable by tracking your results.
- Celebrate reaching milestones along the way, to keep it fun.
- If you miss completing a step, forgive yourself and get back on track the next day.

Committing to do something that is tough or uncomfortable, like exercising or living within your budget, makes us tougher each time we follow through successfully. This positive experience prepares us to commit and follow-through on other tough pursuits that come along later.

In a nutshell: Fully develop your commitment to take action, for without it, all your meticulous planning and goal-setting would remain nothing more than a distant aspiration. Together, desire, motivation, and commitment add to the foundation for becoming the best version of yourself.

In your pursuit of ambitions, these three qualities play a pivotal role. They turn your positive thoughts into real actions, driving you forward and guiding you on a fulfilling journey toward success. As you face challenges on your journey, staying focused and adopting a proactive mindset, driven by self-initiated behavior, become indispensable allies in your quest for progress. These qualities will be thoroughly explored in the next chapter.

JOURNAL PROMPTS

- What are all the possible factors causing you to fear commitment?
- What have these fears kept you from starting or completing, and how has this shaped your life?
- When you don't feel like getting things done or you feel burned out, what usually triggers these feelings? What actions can you take to change your thoughts to minimize or eliminate these feelings?

RECOMMENDED RESOURCES TO LEARN MORE ON THIS TOPIC

Book: *Stop Overthinking* by Nick Trenton

Video: *The Power of Commitment* by Jonathan Jones

25. FOCUS AND PROACTIVITY

The successful warrior is the average man,
with laser-like focus.
— BRUCE LEE

You have a choice in life. You can either live
on-purpose, according to a plan you've set.
Or you can live by accident, reacting to the demands of others.
The first approach is proactive; the second reactive.
— MICHAEL HYATT

Focus – a time management strategy with the goal of elim-inating outside distractions and unnecessary noise so you can do your best work, and get it done faster.

Proactive – creating or controlling a situation by causing something to happen rather than responding to it after it has happened.

What we choose to focus on greatly influences our mindset, emotions, and ultimately, our ability to achieve our goals and lead a fulfilling life. Despite being surrounded by various distractions, it's essential to stay true to our ambitions and consistently direct our attention toward what truly matters. While some people easily ignore distractions, others find it challenging to do so. If you are someone that finds it difficult to look away, this chapter will equip you with the tools to proactively maintain focus and overcome distractions.

Learning to avoid distractions can be a tough challenge, yet it's an essential objective to accomplish. Your attention and focus are vital for effective time management in the short-term and crucial for reaching your long-term goals. Knowing your purpose, the reason why you want to stay focused, helps push you through the tough and tedious parts of accomplishing your goals. We referred to this, in an earlier chapter, as the messy middle of the goal achievement process. That's when our ability to focus is really tested and when it's most needed.

Maintaining focus on a task or practicing mindfulness becomes challenging when you are constantly surrounded by distractions. It is literally at your fingertips as you find yourself scrolling through your social media accounts or viewing the latest news updates. The primary objective of most messaging and communication, whether it's from advertisers, marketers, or other sources, is to seize your attention and prompt you to take action.

Also, it's easy to let your mind wander and start thinking about painful images of the past or fear about the future. These distracting thoughts will prevent you from focusing on what you are trying to accomplish. As previously discussed, negative thoughts can lead to a loss of focus and inaction, becoming a significant obstacle in our journey.

Fortunately, it is possible to improve your mental focus, but it will take effort on your part, as it requires you to improve your habits. Use conscious awareness, or mindfulness, to pay attention to your thoughts and feelings. With practice, learn to block out unhelpful thoughts and urges.

Here are some useful tips for improving your mental focus:

- Motivate yourself to stay mindful by reviewing your purpose statement, your visions, and your goals to keep them top of mind.
- In your planner, write down your daily goals to maintain focus on what you want to accomplish today. Keep them manageable and realistic to avoid feeling overwhelmed.
- Start your day with a simple task to build momentum, then move on your top two or three most important tasks. Completing these will give you the motivation to keep going.
- Before you begin your task, visualize yourself working on it. As we noted previously, "Everything happens twice. First in your mind and then in reality."
- Only focus on one thing at a time. Our brains aren't designed to multitask, so trying to do so leads to poor results.
- Be mindful of potential distractions in your external environment that might lead to procrastination, such as engaging in conversations, grabbing a snack, turning on the television, or checking your phone.
- Make the effort needed to push out internal distractions—thoughts and feelings—running through your mind. Make an effort to stay in the moment.
- Procrastination is a choice. Choose not to.
- If you find yourself struggling with one task, move on to the next, and then return to the previous task once your mind has had more time to think about solutions.
- Take short breaks to temporarily shift your attention to something unrelated and then come back strong a few minutes later.
- Live a healthy lifestyle including 7-8 hours of sleep, daily exercise and eating a nourishing diet to increase your energy.

Even distractions that seem minimal, like an alert on your phone or someone walking by your desk, can get you off your game, so take steps to avoid these concentration breakers.

If you continually find yourself getting sidetracked by unimportant details and are struggling to accomplish your goals, view this as an opportunity to keep practicing. Repeatedly tell yourself you can do this, keep working at it, and you will succeed.

Life doesn't just magically happen. Rather, it is carefully crafted by the decisions you choose to make. Being proactive is without a doubt the most important of the *seven habits*. To be successful in anything you have to be proactive. Even winning the lottery starts with first buying a lottery ticket.[40]

Don't be casual about getting what you want. You never know when an opportunity will come knocking. Stay focused and open to the unexpected, ready to seize the moment.

Keep in mind that encountering challenges is a normal part of life. They can trigger feelings of being overwhelmed, anxious, fearful, or unsure. A reactive individual might resort to blaming others, procrastinating, or quitting. Conversely, A proactive person seeks avenues to turn their struggles into opportunities.

Consider this scenario: many people read self-help books yet fail to implement the suggested changes. They enjoy fantasizing about transformation, but the idea of actual change lies beyond their comfort zone. They continue to lead passive lives and remain stagnant. Please, don't fall into this category. Instead, be the individual who possesses the courage to take action, patiently awaits opportunities, and springs into action when they arise. Fight for your desires.

Proactive behavior is what separates the person who retires comfortably at 50 from the person who can't afford to retire at 65. Being proactive means making thoughtful financial decisions early in life, which leads to a secure and stress-free

---

40 Stephen R. Covey, *The 7 Habits of Highly Effective People*, 2013.

retirement. On the other hand, a lack of proactivity may lead to financial constraints and a delayed retirement.

As a pharmacist, I view it as proactive behavior when a patient consistently takes their medication every day to keep their blood pressure under control, as opposed to someone who only takes it when they feel unwell due to their blood pressure soaring. Consequently, the patient who maintains consistent medication adherence is less likely to end up in the hospital.

Here are a few suggestions for increasing your proactive behavior:

1. Your language matters. Pay attention to how you talk to yourself. Negative self-talk, such as telling yourself why you can't do something, will sabotage your efforts.
2. Look for solutions rather than dwelling on problems. What can you learn from adversity, and how can you leverage it to grow and handle the problem better next time? Proactive people are masters at problem-solving.
3. Focus on what you can control, and that is yourself. Think positive, have confidence, and develop a plan to become more proactive. It is a skill, so keep practicing.
4. Take action to change a situation or habit that no longer serves you.

In a nutshell: In this chapter, we've learned how focus and proactivity play a crucial role in achieving a successful and fulfilling life. Being proactive means thinking ahead, taking control of what we can, and making plans to address challenges, while saving us valuable time and resources by preventing minor issues from becoming larger concerns.

Now equipped with focus and proactivity in our toolkit, we know that being prepared to avoid distractions and overcome obstacles is essential for staying on track. In the next chapter, we'll explore the significance of willpower and self-discipline for moving past the messy middle.

JOURNAL PROMPTS

- During a typical day, which distractions divert your attention from mindful thoughts and work focus? How much time each day do you find yourself acting mindlessly? What steps can you take to minimize these distractions?
- Write down any foreseeable obstacles or challenges related to each of your goals. Highlight the ones within your control, such as making excuses for not taking action. Next, brainstorm potential solutions or alternative approaches for each of these challenges.
- Create a list of the tasks you truly want to accomplish this month.

RECOMMENDED RESOURCES
TO LEARN MORE ON THIS TOPIC

Book: *Focus* by Daniel Goleman

Book: *Hyperfocus* by Chris Bailey

Video: *How to Get Your Brain to Focus* by Chris Bailey

Podcast: *Be Less Reactive and More Proactive* on Harvard Business Review Ideacast

26. WILLPOWER AND SELF-DISCIPLINE

Talent without discipline is just wasted opportunity.
— ZIG ZIGLAR

The difference between a successful person and others is not a lack of strength, not a lack of knowledge, but rather a lack of will.
— VINCE LOMBARDI

Willpower – the ability to resist instant gratification in order to achieve long-term goals.

Self-discipline – the ability to control one's feelings and overcome one's weaknesses; the ability to pursue what one thinks is right despite temptations to abandon it.

Our lives are significantly affected by our ability—or inability—to attain goals and find success in various areas of life. Whether it's personal growth, career aspirations, or better relationships, self-discipline plays a crucial role in reaching our goals and driving us forward. Research even suggests that willpower might be a stronger predictor of success than IQ. Adding willpower and self-discipline to our toolkit is essential for turning dreams into reality.[41]

The numerous self-help books available at airport bookstores suggest that many of us face challenges in enhancing our discipline and fortifying our willpower. Willpower is your ability to control your unhelpful thoughts, feelings, and behavior, especially in the face of temptation. It is another skill that you can learn to improve with practice. We can fulfill our long-term goals more efficiently when we can resist short-term temptations.

Strengthening your willpower helps you rein in impulses and cravings, which enables you to make proactive choices that guide you on your path to success. If you've felt frustrated due to procrastination, lack of progress on your goals, or a sense of being unable to control your actions, you may be grappling with self-discipline challenges. Self-discipline is characterized by structure, careful planning, and consistency, while willpower involves sudden, momentary bursts of focused energy. I view these as complimentary skills.

Have you ever told yourself, "If only I had more willpower, I could put an end to procrastination, consistently save for retirement, adhere to an exercise routine, and break free from vices like overeating or smoking cigarettes"?

Unhealthy impulsive actions that may seem to be minor or inconsequential decisions, like giving in to a craving and eating some donuts brought in by a co-worker, can put you on a road that is difficult to exit. The choices might seem small at the time, but once you start building momentum in the wrong direction, reversing course becomes a difficult struggle.

To fight impulses and distractions, it's important to have the willpower to pause and think before you act. Consider whether your action brings you closer to, or farther from, your

---

41 Charles Duhigg, *The Power of Habit*, 2014.

goals. Remind yourself why you have chosen your goals and the benefits you will gain from reaching them.

Here are additional methods I've come across that can strengthen both your self-discipline and willpower:

- When confronted with a temptation, whether it's the desire to eat, drink, or buy something you don't really need, try this tactic: Shift your gaze or physically eliminate the temptation from your surroundings. If that's not feasible, step away temporarily from the temptation.
- Prioritize getting sufficient sleep. Sleep-deprived people are more susceptible to giving in to impulses, have reduced focus, and tend to make risky decisions.
- Train your self-discipline by engaging in actions that deviate from your routine, particularly those you might initially prefer to avoid. For instance, if you're not accustomed to it, make it a practice to switch off the lights every time you exit a room.
- Pay attention to your thoughts and emotions when you feel tempted to yield to an impulse.
- Develop the resolve to persist despite occasional setbacks. Learn to endure short-term discomfort and resist surrendering to distractions. Tell yourself, "This is important for my progress, and a little discomfort won't stop me ." Pause for a moment, regain your refocus, and reaffirm your commitment. Once we recognize temptation for what it is, we can hopefully steer clear of it or divert our attention elsewhere.
- Let your actions speak for you. While others might provoke you with their words, you can adopt the discipline to respond thoughtfully instead of impulsively.
- Create a well thought-out strategy for handling temptations and visualize yourself actively choosing to avoid them. Repeat this mental exercise regularly.

The first point in the above list brings to mind The Marshmallow Test. This test evaluated the capability of young children to delay gratification, offering them a choice between receiving an immediate treat or waiting for even more treats later. Kids who exhibited more self-control during the test achieved better results in various aspects of life as they grew up. The study emphasizes the connection between self-discipline and delayed gratification in achieving long-term success.[42]

Learning self-discipline and willpower early in your adult life will help you for decades to come, and it is something you can continue to practice as you age. Another definition I came across explains that willpower helps occasionally, and self-discipline helps all the time. Willpower provides the push and strength for immediate action, while self-discipline empowers you with the endurance, patience, and strength needed to persist in your plans and actions until you achieve success.

Self-discipline and willpower involve conscious choice to act wisely. Progressing toward your goals involves taking deliberate, incremental steps that are in harmony with your plan. The decision to opt for an apple over a donut, or to leave for a workout instead of checking your Facebook page, showcases these skills. Demonstrations of self-discipline occur when we follow our financial security plan, depositing extra money into savings instead of impulsively buying yet another pair of shoes.

In the event of a misstep, practice self-forgiveness and recommit to your objective. Reflect on your thoughts and emotions after making a choice that diverted you from your goal; this introspection can guide better decisions in the future. Similarly, if you momentarily deviate from your plans or goals, exercising self-discipline helps you regain your footing. We all experience setbacks, but they should be brief detours rather than a complete change of direction. Remember, the main goal

---

42 Walter Mischel, *The Marshmallow Test*, 2015.

is to become the person you picture yourself as, which requires feeling empowered, staying committed, and steering your life in the right direction.

I also suggest enhancing your self-discipline by incorporating forms of accountability. Share your intentions with your support network, requesting follow-up calls to discuss progress. Also, build discipline by trying something new that slightly intimidates you. For instance, despite not considering myself athletic, I recently signed up for several pickleball lessons. I attended every session even after a rough fall in the very first class. Attempting new challenges injects vitality and balance into your life.

In a nutshell: Mastering willpower and self-discipline involves effective strategies such as setting priorities and thinking before acting. These skills give you control over your actions and help you break free from detrimental habits that hold you back. With these tools you'll make choices that align with your goals and purpose.

Despite the acknowledged importance of these skills, only a few invest the necessary effort to nurture them. Making steady progress, even in the face of fear, demands courage, confidence, and resilience. These qualities will be boldly explored in the next chapter.

JOURNAL PROMPTS

- List two or three unhelpful habits that you can improve with greater willpower. Set a goal to change one of these habits.
- For the next several days, be mindful of the temptations you encounter that challenge your self-control. Make a note of what these temptations are, how they influence your thoughts and emotions, and whether you successfully avoided giving in to them.

RECOMMENDED RESOURCES TO LEARN MORE ON THIS TOPIC

Book: *Willpower: Rediscovering the Greatest Human Strength* by Roy F. Baumeister and John Tierney

Book: *The Science of Self-Discipline* by Peter Hollins

Video: *The Five Levels of Self-Discipline* by Thomas Frank

Podcast: *Everyday Discipline* by Brent Kocal

27. COURAGE, CONFIDENCE, AND RESILIENCE

*Courage is going from failure
to failure without losing enthusiasm.*
— WINSTON CHURCHILL

*Resilience is all about being able to overcome
the unexpected. The goal of resilience is to thrive.*
— JAMAIS CASCIO

Courage – the ability to do something that is frightening.

Resilience – the capacity to withstand or to recover quickly from difficulties; toughness.

Confidence – the unwavering belief in your ability to face life's challenges, take decisive action, and succeed.

As we've previously discussed, the pursuit of our goals frequently clashes with our immediate impulses. Alongside focus, proactivity, and other skills we've covered, courage, confidence, and resilience are equally essential. These qualities enable us to withstand those impulses and choose actions that contribute to our long-term welfare. To translate positive thoughts into positive feelings and, eventually, purposeful actions to enrich our lives, we must actively practice and develop these skills.

Growing your courage can help you tackle risks and achieve positive outcomes, yet overcoming your fears demands effort. Essentially, courage involves careful evaluation of risks and rewards, followed by action despite the inevitable presence of fear.

Resilience, often referred to as mental toughness, encompasses a range of values, attitudes, behaviors, emotions, and mindsets. It empowers you to persevere and conquer obstacles, adversity, or pressure. It also enables you to maintain focus and motivation during favorable times, ensuring consistent achievement of your goals.

Many of us grapple with confidence, regardless of our achievements or accomplishments. Consider an individual with multiple degrees and a couple of published books, yet lacking the confidence to present at a meeting. They feel apprehensive about appearing inept and terrified of potential mockery, likely related to the impostor syndrome we discussed in a previous chapter. Courage involves feeling afraid but proceeding anyway. Confidence is a potent ally, as long as it's balanced with wisdom and self-restraint.

Learning from experience, I've come to realize that the fear of worrying about potential mishaps or failure often exceeds the actual challenges you encounter when you take action. It's important to understand that failure is merely an event; it doesn't define you're identity.

Confronting challenges is a natural aspect of life. A crucial factor that distinguishes those who achieve their goals from those who give up is how they react to these challenges. You can either allow pessimistic thoughts and emotions to immobilize you with fear and self-doubt, or you can counteract them by choosing to confront the challenge and push ahead.

Those individuals who struggle to rebound from adversity tend to internalize failure and eventually abandon their efforts. Although everyone faces difficulties, challenges, and setbacks, it's our resilience that determines whether we'll persevere and grow stronger, or submit to defeat.

Common obstacles that threaten the development of resilience include:

- self-pity—indulging in negativity;
- self-doubt—feeling immobilized by insecurity;
- your inner critic—the negative voice in your mind;
- fear—a potent emotion that convinces you that action will be harmful;
- laziness—unwillingness to put in effort or expend the energy required to persevere;
- perfectionism—waiting for everything to line up perfectly before taking action;
- emotionalism—feeling overwhelmed by discouragement and unable to move forward;
- self-limiting beliefs—false notions about your capabilities;
- burnout syndrome—mental or physical exhaustion due to excessive stress;
- not being proactive—lacking readiness to respond when faced with adversity.

In order to develop resilience and navigate challenges effectively, it's essential to recognize and overcome these common obstacles that can constrain your progress and growth.

Keep in mind that it's completely acceptable to quit something if you realize that it no longer resonates with you. It might have lost its significance, or perhaps an opportunity that better reflects your aspirations has emerged. This is distinct from quitting because you're unable to rise to the challenge.

Choosing to be passive, or giving into apathy, is like asking "What is going to happen to me?" On the other hand, choosing courage is asking "What action am I going to take?" It's your choice to act brave.[43]

When faced with adversity, a reactive person tends to retreat and place blame on the world for their issues, often asking, "Why me?" The reality is that no one is going to rescue you. It's your responsibility to turn your setbacks into victories.

The reassuring fact is that courage, or mental toughness, can be developed and strengthened through practice. It guides you to turn challenges into achievements, enhancing your self-confidence when facing adversity, uncertainty, and misfortune.

Numerous tips exist to enhance your mental resilience, and the good news is that you're already familiar with most of these from having read previous chapters in this book:

- Prioritize self-care: eat healthy, stay hydrated, exercise, and ensure a restful night's sleep to boost your energy levels.
- Develop positive self-perception and practice constructive self-talk leading to positive emotions and behaviors—the familiar cognitive triangle at work.
- Maintain an organized and clean environment to reduce mental stress.
- Refrain from comparing yourself to others. Don't let fear of what others might think keep you from taking a risk and doing what's right for you. Walk your own path.
- Surround yourself with positive people. Ask your support group for advice when needed.
- Regularly engage in activities where you excel, to build your self-assurance.

---

43 Ryan Holiday, *Courage Is Calling*, 2021.

- Set achievable goals with manageable steps.
- Envision the worst-case scenario and devise a survival plan if it were to occur.
- Employ a mindset of deferred gratification to maintain focus on long-term objectives.
- Should you feel overwhelmed, scale down your actions while maintaining forward momentum.

One of the best pieces of advice I've encountered for conquering your fears is to anticipate their arrival. And when they do arise, consider addressing them as a motivating challenge. Remind yourself that there are people relying on you to finish this task because your achievement will provide them with valuable assistance in their endeavors. The fulfillment derived from helping others is universally rewarding. That advice kept me going when I encountered many roadblocks while writing this book.

You have the power to choose how you feel about yourself and the way you want to live your life. So, make the choice to keep going after your goals and remain confident that you can handle whatever happens, whether it's good or not-so-good. This bravery gives you the ability to keep learning and growing all the time. It's the energy that lets you take bold actions even when you're not sure how things will turn out. It helps you wholeheartedly work toward making your vision board dreams a reality. Take ownership and rewrite your narrative.

In a nutshell: In this chapter, we've learned that courage, confidence, and resilience are essential in how we handle life's challenges. While we can't control everything that happens, we can control how we react. Instead of giving up when things get tough, tap your courage and sense of purpose to persevere.

Rather than fearing failure, let your bigger fear be never taking a shot. Learn from past mistakes and use them as valuable lessons to drive improvement. Venture beyond your comfort zone and embrace fresh opportunities.

With newfound courage, confidence, and resilience, you'll make wiser choices concerning your health, relationships, time, and overall wellbeing. Moving forward, our focus turns to seizing control of your life through sound decision-making and autonomy.

JOURNAL PROMPTS

• What are some examples of everyday courage in your life—those smaller, equally important ways you've shown up for yourself and others?
• In what areas of your life would you like to have more courage right now? Consider both your personal and professional life. What actions could you take to get unstuck?
• Make a list of everything you have achieved that required self-confidence and courage. This could include the A grade you earned in a challenging math class, the game you contributed to your team's victory, and the raise you received after confidently requesting it.

RECOMMENDED RESOURCES TO LEARN MORE ON THIS TOPIC

Book: *Option B: Facing Adversity, Building Resilience, and Finding Joy* by Sheryl Sandberg and Adam Grant

Book: *The Magic of Thinking Big* by David J. Schwartz

Video: Courage—Best Motivational Video Speeches Compilation by Motiversity

Podcast: Courageous Self-Confidence with Samuel Hatton

28. DECISION-MAKING AND AUTONOMY

Not making a decision is actually a decision.
It's the decision to stay the same.
— LYSA TERKEURST

Good decisions come from experience.
Experience comes from making bad decisions.
— MARK TWAIN

Decision-making – choosing between two or more courses of action.

Personal autonomy – the feeling of freedom or control over one's life and self.

Each day, we find ourselves making decisions, some of which come naturally and require little contemplation. Deciding what to wear, what to eat, or which route to take to work may be routine choices that don't significantly impact our lives. However, in this chapter, we will explore the process of making wiser choices with enduring benefits and consequences, as we consider the significance of major, more complicated, decision-making and autonomy.

People who tend to over-think every detail of their lives may find it difficult to make long-term decisions. They can feel overwhelmed by the decision-making process and get stuck in it, leading them to make the wrong choices in life.

We often end up making bad decisions due to various reasons:

- overconfidence—we think we know everything, but we do not;
- feeling overwhelmed—too many choices can stress us out;
- lack of confidence—we plan a lot but struggle to take action;
- feeling like it doesn't matter—we downplay the decision's importance;
- present bias—we choose what feels good now, not what's best for later;
- perfectionism—it makes us freeze and miss chances.

Every decision we make carries either positive or negative consequences. Relying on hope or making impulsive choices aren't approaches I recommend for addressing significant decisions that affect our future. Making snap decisions without clear thinking can lead to hardship, leaving us wondering, "How did I end up here?"

Making decisions can sometimes feel like navigating a maze of complexity. It's easy to trick ourselves into believing that every choice we've made was the right one, even when things didn't go as planned. We want to hold onto the idea that we're great decision-makers, so when life takes unexpected turns, we tend to blame external factors instead of accepting our own role in it. This tangled mix of past choices and present realities can make decision-making even trickier, as we try to balance taking responsibility while acknowledging life's uncertainties.

Difficulty in making decisions can also occur from a lack of clarity around the problem, being unclear about our priorities, not seeing all possibilities, and then struggling to evaluate our options. However, there's a solution. Implementing a structured decision-making process can help us overcome these obstacles and streamline our choices, making the decision-making journey much smoother and more effective.

Past unwise decisions can cast long shadows over our lives, if we let them. Often, these choices were made without a deep understanding of ourselves. By practicing self-reflection and gaining insights into our identity and desires, we lay the groundwork for wiser choices ahead. To ensure we are making meaningful choices with positive, long-lasting benefits that keep us on our true path, building up our decision-making skills is crucial.

Adopting a systematic approach to decision-making enables us to make effective choices that move us toward our goals. While it might seem like a smart decision involves weighing pros and cons and living with the outcomes, the reality is more intricate. Our choices are shaped by various factors including biases, logical errors, ingrained emotions, and memories, which can sometimes lead us astray.

It's important to do everything possible to ensure our decisions are well-informed. With each significant choice we face—whether it's accepting a job offer, starting or ending a relationship, or making a significant relocation—we are trading one path for another, embracing change while letting go of something else. We are responsible for examining past decisions that didn't yield desired outcomes, learning from them to avoid repeating mistakes, and thereby enhancing our decision-making mastery.

Before examining the components of a sound decision-making process, it's important to point out life's unpredictability. Achieving 100% certainty in our choices is elusive, as we can't predict every future development. Certainty doesn't factor into decision-making; however, you are accountable for the choices you make in life.

Here's a reliable process for making well-informed decisions:

- Begin by understanding your purpose, passions, values, and goals. Align your choices with these guiding principles. Will your decision move you closer to your objectives or push you farther away?
- Recognize that there is no perfect choice. Every decision carries unknown consequences. For lower-risk options, spend less time deliberating.
- Don't let the fear of making the wrong choice and experiencing regret cause procrastination and missed opportunities. If your decision doesn't produce the desired results, consider it an opportunity for learning and growth.
- Avoid confining yourself to a binary choice (A or B). Often alternative solutions lie in the gray area, offering potentially superior outcomes.
- Seek advice from your support network, but weigh it carefully. Ultimately, you must determine what aligns best with your needs.
- Once you've made a decision, take decisive action. This is the only way to move forward. Trust in your abilities to overcome any challenges that may arise.

Remember, the decision-making process doesn't guarantee certainty, but it does empower you to navigate life's choices with a thoughtful and purposeful approach. Devoting time and thought to decisions with significant potential consequences is an immensely valuable use of your time. Your choices determine the overall quality of your life and the extent of your success.

However, if you are struggling to make a decision or move

forward due to current challenges, then now might not be the best time to act. It's alright to put off a decision for a while until things are better. This is different from delaying because you're scared or unsure.

In decision-making, we utilize two distinct types of thinking: fast thinking and slow thinking. Fast thinking is employed in quick, automatic responses, such as when driving in heavy traffic. On the other hand, slow thinking is applied when we have more time to deliberate and consider various options, like when choosing a new car or selecting a college to attend.[44]

It's important not to use fast thinking for decisions that require slow thinking. For best results, in these situations, learn to delay decisions until you have time to think slow. Sit in solitude and calm your mind until you feel confident and ready to decide what is in your own best interest.

Remember, to experience joy and fulfillment, you need to have the autonomy to act in your own best interest. Autonomy permits you to make independent decisions that align with your personal values and goals, instead of being coerced by external forces. No one wants to feel like a marionette with someone or something else pulling on our strings.

Many people are servants to the pressures or cravings of an addiction, fears, or likes on social media. If you feel forced to stay with a job you hate because of bills hanging over your head every month, you have reduced autonomy. I have seen pharmacy patients experience feelings of depression and helplessness due to having a low level of autonomy in their life. Many of them had a spouse or caregiver making their decisions for them.

Acting with autonomy gives you the freedom to choose from alternative courses of action. You get to decide about increasing your knowledge, improving your skills, and having responsibility for your own actions. This independence is vital

44 Daniel Kahneman, *Thinking, Fast and Slow*, 2013.

in many ways. People who can engage in autonomous behavior are more likely to succeed at work, achieve their academic goals, and feel happier in general.

Increasing your autonomy won't just happen on its own. It takes courage and positive energy to look deep within yourself and start to take responsibility for your situation in life. Don't be like Kevin, a character in the TV show Bloodline, who said, "Sometimes I feel I just let life take me wherever it wanted. I didn't take any responsibility. I just kind of coasted." If you want to have more autonomy, be clear about what you want and take the steps needed to get it.

In a nutshell: Discover the power of autonomy - take charge of *what* you do, *when* you do it, *how* you do it, and *whom* you do it with. Practice making your own decisions and feel the empowerment and control it brings to your life. As you act autonomously, you'll conquer challenges, make important choices, and achieve a sense of accomplishment. Direct your focus toward your vision of your future self to guide you in making decisions that will be beneficial in the long-run, while also avoiding impulsive choices.

With improved decision-making and greater autonomy, you'll experience higher levels of wellbeing, stronger relationships, and a more meaningful life, while reducing anxiety and depression. In the next chapter we'll explore a skill considered the most crucial of all – effective communication. Effective communication skills will profoundly benefit both your career and personal life.

JOURNAL PROMPTS

- What decisions have been occupying your thoughts? These choices could pertain to work, finances, self-care, or relationships. How can you gather additional information to make an informed choice? How can you ensure this decision aligns with your life purpose?
- What are the pros and cons of each option you are considering?
- What is your current process for making decisions and how can you improve it?

RECOMMENDED RESOURCE
TO LEARN MORE ON THIS TOPIC

Book: *Don't Overthink It* by Anne Bogel

Book: *Thinking, Fast and Slow* by Daniel Kahneman

Book: *Drive* by Daniel H. Pink

Podcast: "How to Make Better Decisions" on *The Science of Happiness* podcast by Judge Jeremy Fogle

Blog: "What Is Autonomy and Why Is It So Difficult to Achieve?" by John A Johnson on Psychologytoday.com

29. COMMUNICATION SKILLS

*Nothing in life is more important than
the ability to communicate effectively.*
— GERALD R. FORD

*The most important thing in communication
is hearing what isn't said.*
— PETER DRUCKER

Communication – sending and receiving messages through
verbal and non-verbal means.

**Being able to communicate effectively is the most important of
all life skills.**[45] Communication is more than just exchanging
information, like deciding who walks the dog. It's the key to
overcoming challenges, embracing change, and fostering meaningful connections in all areas of life. From family talks to work
collaborations and social encounters, being a great communicator
will enable you to listen, speak, observe, and empathize with
others. So, let's unlock your communication potential.

---

45 John C. Maxwell, *Everyone Communicates Few Connect*, 2010.

Your ability to communicate is an important tool in the pursuit of your career goals. It is a key skill for success. When you deliver a presentation at work, brainstorm with your co-workers, address a problem with your boss, or confirm details with a client about their project, you use communication skills. They're an essential part of developing positive professional relationships.

Outside of work, good communication is equally important for advancing positive social interactions with friends, family, and when meeting new people. We love connecting with other people because it brings us joy. Good communication also helps us resolve conflicts.

Communication skills can be grouped into four categories. Let's take a closer look at each type and see how they play a role in our interactions:

1. Written communication. Writing is one of the more traditional aspects of communication. We frequently write as part of our job and in our personal life—communicating via email and messenger apps, as well as in more formal documents like project reports and white papers. Conveying information clearly, concisely, and with an accurate tone of voice, is an important part of written communication.

2. Verbal communication. Communicating verbally is how many of us share information with those nearby or when using the phone. This can be informal, such as chatting with co-workers about an upcoming sales meeting, or more formal, such as meeting with your manager to discuss your performance. Outside of work, we have conversations at the dinner table and in social situations. Taking time to actively listen when someone else is talking is also an important part of verbal communication.

3. Non-verbal communication. You communicate messages non-verbally through your body language, eye contact, and overall demeanor. You can express yourself non-verbally by using appropriate facial expressions, nodding, and making good eye contact. Verbal and non-verbal communication must be in sync to convey a clear message. I remember learning in an MBA communications class that 93% of communication is non-verbal, so this is certainly an important skill to learn and practice.

4. Visual communication. Lastly, visual communication is when we use visual elements to convey a message, inspire change, or evoke emotion using images, graphs, charts, and other non-written means to share information. This type of communication is also on display when your meal is set in front of you at a restaurant. Good presentation upgrades the dish. Often, visuals may accompany one of the other three communication types.

Improving your communication skills can help you achieve your goals more effectively. If you want to advance your career or grow a relationship, you need to have good communication skills. It's a skill used throughout life. Here are some suggestions you can practice for improving your communication abilities.

Practice active listening. Pay attention and concentrate on what the other person is saying. Use eye contact, mirroring, smiling, and leaning in. Ask good questions, ask for clarification, and summarize back to them. Listen with all your senses and ignore distractions.

Focus on non-verbal communication. Maintain good eye contact when listening and responding. Use appropriate facial expressions. Use a vocal tone that matches what is being said. Practice using good posture when communicating. Take pride in your appearance wherever you go in public or during a teleconference. Maintain appropriate personal space. Watch someone you feel is a good communicator and emulate their style to help you improve.

Manage your emotions. Take a pause before you overreact. Imagine what message you are conveying when you overreact and unload on someone due to the awful day you're having. If you communicate a strong negative emotion, explain how you're feeling, accept responsibility for your emotions, and thank the other person for listening.

Seek feedback on your skill level. Consider what you aim to achieve before asking for input. Prepare well-formulated, open-ended questions and identify the appropriate individuals to ask. Address them by name and ask them what they think, attentively listening to their answers. Demonstrate your commitment to their feedback by taking notes on the information shared. Finally, reflect on the feedback, review your approach, and respond with grace and respect.

Practice public speaking. Sign up for a program in your area so you can practice in front of a live audience. Toastmasters International is excellent for increasing your confidence and ability. Record your talk. Don't memorize it or read it directly from a sheet of paper or your phone. Visualize yourself giving a successful talk as part of your preparation. Believe in yourself and your abilities.

Develop a filter. Only say or write what is beneficial to the listener or reader. Be sure it is not confidential. Make sure that what you communicate is true. Don't be a gossip.

In a nutshell: In learning communication skills, remember to be attentive and considerate when interacting with others. Give them your full attention and thoughtfully consider their words. Value their input and embrace different perspectives to enrich your understanding. Every conversation is an opportunity to learn and grow.

If you are willing to put yourself out there and be vulnerable, it can lead to a life-changing conversation. We're all trying to be heard and understood. Effective communication paves the way to successful outcomes while poor communication leads to confusion and chaos.

As we journey toward self-improvement, accountability plays a vital role in achieving our goals. It keeps us motivated and focused on what truly matters. In the next chapter, we'll explore the benefits of accountability and the potential of a support network.

JOURNAL PROMPTS

- On a scale of 1–10, how would you rate your communication skills? What are your strengths? What are some areas that need a little improvement?
- How does your self-confidence impact your communication?
- How can you improve your active listening skills?
- What are some things you find difficult to communicate? Why?
- How do you usually communicate when you're feeling angry, sad, or happy?

RECOMMENDED RESOURCES TO LEARN MORE ON THIS TOPIC

Book: *Communication Skills Training* by James W. Williams

Book: *How to Talk to Anyone Effectively* by Daniel J. Bellow

Video: *The Power of Communication* by Nina Legath

Podcast: *The Communication Guys Podcast* by Tim Downs and Dr. Tom Barrett

Tip: Invest in your future. Sign up today for a program like Toastmasters or take a Dale Carnegie course. Taking the time and investing some money to advance your career and improve your personal life will be a decision you won't regret.

30. ACCOUNTABILITY AND SUPPORT NETWORK

Personal Accountability – accepting responsibility for your life—everything in your life.

Accountability Partner – someone you can count on to offer encouragement and support.

Support Network – people in your life who help you achieve your goals; "your team."

How's your journey going so far? We've covered various empowering skills to conquer negativity and attain greater success in life. With a clear purpose guiding you, a well-thought-out plan brimming with SMART goals, and consistent strides toward your vision, you're well on your way. Are you witnessing the outcomes you envisioned? If not, pause for a moment to reflect on a possible reason. Are you fully taking responsibility for the results stemming from your thoughts, emotions, and actions?

In this chapter, we'll explore how to be more accountable for both positive and negative outcomes. Embracing accountability enhances personal growth and self-awareness. By taking ownership of your actions and choices, you take the time to measure results, make adjustments when necessary, and celebrate your successes. This commitment leads you to reach new heights in your journey.

Acting with personal accountability means asking yourself, "What can I do to make this better?" and, "What can I learn from this mistake?" Every setback should be viewed as an opportunity to come back stronger and smarter than before. But you will struggle to do that if you are not accepting full responsibility for your choices, actions, and their outcomes.

Also, when you have a way to measure your progress you are more likely to stay motivated and achieve your goals. Monitoring your progress helps you understand how well you are doing and where you can improve. Some outcome measurements are obvious, such as tracking your weight when you are dieting. However, when you are improving other habits, skills, and mindsets, it's important to identify what you can measure. Consider tracking the number of tasks completed, how much time something took, achieving milestones, or beating deadlines.

I assumed responsibility for my actions and outcomes by conquering my fear of initiating and sustaining a fitness routine. Despite past failed attempts driven by excessive expectations and excuses, such as busyness or weather conditions, I recognized the need for a mindset shift. Believing in myself and grasping the importance of this goal in fulfilling my purpose, I felt assured of my potential for success. Taking ownership of the outcome, tracking my progress, and with a little support from my friends, I found myself compelled to take the necessary steps toward achieving my goal.

This time, I adopted a gradual approach. I chose to start with a manageable workout and then slowly escalate the level of challenge. I began by simply strolling around the block at a consistent time each day—after all, it was written on my daily planner! The routine felt easy, boosting my self-esteem with each completion. Before long, missing a day felt uncomfortable. I documented my progress with brief notes in my planner, recording the distance, step count, and duration. Rather than seeking excuses, I focused on reasons I could accomplish this.

Within a month or two, walking became an ingrained habit. It was no longer a matter of deciding if I felt like it; I expected it of myself. Gradually, I expanded my walking distance and increased the pace. After half a year of consistent walking and reaching a daily goal of 10,000 steps, I felt ready to incorporate resistance training twice a week.

With guidance from a trainer, I was introduced to effective exercises for building strength, balance, and muscle. I began this phase slowly as well, starting with very light weights and a few exercises. Over time, I methodically increased the weight and repetitions, incorporating additional weight-bearing exercises. Today, one year later, I lift much heavier weights and execute the maximum number of repetitions advised by the trainer. The routine is now firmly established on my Wednesdays and Saturdays, thoughtfully documented in my planner, along with the weights and repetitions.

I attribute the success of this endeavor to my newfound accountability mindset, emphasizing gradual progress and outcome measurement. Beyond the satisfaction of witnessing improvement, my motivation is fueled by my larger purpose of enhancing my quality of life. Exercising has become my daily dose of happiness.

If you find yourself struggling to make progress with your goals, consider how you can enhance your accountability. When you fall short of completing a planned task, take a moment to identify what sabotaged you, learn from the experience, adjust your approach slightly, and continue moving forward. Don't be disheartened and avoid seeking excuses to give up. I once heard someone mention that they spent 60 minutes preparing for a relatively short task. Once they recognized this inefficiency, they managed to cut their preparation time down to just 10 minutes, while still accomplishing the task effectively.

Celebrating your achievements, whether with a triumphant fist pump or a relaxing 30-minute soak in a soothing bath, is an excellent way to maintain motivation. You can also consider some form of punishment, like pledging a donation to a cause you don't favor when failing to meet a goal, to enhance personal accountability. Just ensure that the reward or punishment corresponds to the goal, keeping your progress alive and well.

You might also document your success with a photo on your vision board to remind yourself of how great it felt to reach a goal or milestone. A snapshot of you triumphantly crossing the finish line at the 5K run will make you feel proud! Also use positive self-talk with plenty of praise, compliments, and encouragement, as you complete each step in the process or finish a chore. A couple of fist pumps!

Acting accountable is foundational for long-term success. And remember, there is no losing. There is only winning and learning. Understand that as soon as you think you have it all figured out, something will change, and you will end up facing a new obstacle. It could be an ankle sprain or something more serious that causes you to adjust your plans. Life never progresses in a straight line.

Assuming personal accountability can significantly enhance the satisfaction and enjoyment you experience in life.[46] While it's valuable to learn from books like *Rise Above the Rut* and other self-help books, it's even more crucial to put that knowledge into action and hold yourself responsible for your outcomes.

Consider these tips to strengthen your personal accountability:

- Make a firm commitment: Clearly define your aspirations and pledge to yourself to achieve them.
- Seek clarity: Have a precise understanding of expectations and required actions.
- Set SMART goals: Establish goals that are specific, measurable, achievable, relevant and timebound.
- Avoid blame: Take ownership of your actions and refrain from attributing them to others or to external circumstances.
- Cultivate self-accountability: Regularly monitor your progress and reflect on your actions and outcomes to ensure consistent growth and improvement.
- Partner with an accountability ally: Identify someone who can support you and help you stay on track when needed.

Now, let's dig into the significance of this final tip - partnering with an accountability ally. To unlock your full potential, it's incredibly beneficial to surround yourself with individuals who offer support and guidance. These partners can be friends, family members, colleagues, co-workers, fellow organization members, mentors, or even a personal coach you decide to enlist.

Often in life, we find ourselves facing stressful situations that seem more manageable with a companion by our side. A supportive friend stands as a pillar, ready to brave even the

---

46 John G. Miller, *QBQ!*, 2004.

toughest challenges alongside you. However, it's important to note that this doesn't mean they'll blindly follow your lead.

A genuine supporter is equipped to aid you in decision-making by objectively evaluating the pros and cons of your choices. They may even voice their disagreement if they believe your path is unwise. Regardless of your decision , they'll stand by you, offering their unwavering support. A true partner lacks judgment and hidden agendas; their care for you is sincere and transparent.

Different goals might necessitate distinct support partners. For instance, you might seek one person's assistance in navigating a career change and another's for achieving financial milestones. This marks the initiation of a support network, a circle of individuals you can rely on to inspire progress in various aspects of your life.

This very notion prompted me to join the Nonfiction Authors Association, a community of passionate and skilled writers, authors, publishers, editors, and book marketers. Drawing from this network, I've not only gained knowledge, but also maintained motivation throughout the writing journey, thanks to the support of numerous members.

To foster a thriving network, it's crucial for you to contribute value by aligning with their vision or mission. This can manifest through acts of compassion, generosity, and guidance based on your areas of expertise. Mutual benefit is key, and a balanced exchange within the relationship is essential.

Both accountability partners and support networks play pivotal roles in propelling you toward success. Regularly nurturing and upholding these relationships is vital for their enduring strength. Neglecting them risks deterioration, and rebuilding or replacing them can prove exceptionally challenging.

Here are a few recommendations for maximizing the value you receive and contribute within a support network:

- Compose concise personal messages to introduce yourself to fellow members.
- Engage with individuals from various levels within an organization to expand your network.
- Participate in groups or forums aligned with your interests and initiate introductions with other members.
- Seek guidance when needed and extend your assistance when others reach out.
- Consider starting your own blog to share valuable insights and expertise that can be helpful to others.

In a nutshell: Personal accountability means taking full responsibility for your actions. No more making excuses or evading tasks; instead, you approach them with fervent determination and a hunger for success. This empowers you to build willpower, set goals, make strides, conquer obstacles, and ultimately achieve success. As you pursue your goals, having inspiring accountability partners and a supportive network can significantly boost motivation, provide guidance, and aid in overcoming challenges across various aspects of your life.

Have you noticed signs that you're breaking free from stagnation? The sense of being trapped in the same monotonous routine and experiencing unhappiness is gradually dissipating. In the next and final chapter of Step 3: Achieve Consistent Progress, we'll explore the unmistakable indicators of positive transformation and growth, revealing the remarkable success that you might never have dared to envision.

JOURNAL PROMPTS

- Write down a list of five actions or goals that you haven't taken responsibility for completing recently.
- How do you believe accountability and responsibility can enhance your life and assist you in the process of self-discovery?
- Solicit specific feedback from colleagues regarding the quality of your work, and from friends and family regarding your performance in personal matters. Develop a plan to improve in these areas, and establish metrics for gauging your progress, like follow-ups with those who provided input. Express gratitude for their advice.

RECOMMENDED RESOURCES TO LEARN MORE ON THIS TOPIC

Book: *Making Accountable Decisions* by Sam Silverstein

Book: *Connect* by David L. Bradford and Carole Robin

Video: *Check Yourself: Accountability* by Charlie Johnson

Tip: Create profiles on one or two apps like Facebook, LinkedIn, and Meetup to look for groups with members who hold similar interests to you. Join and see what you can learn and contribute.

31. ARE YOU RISING ABOVE THE RUT?

It's better to have tried and failed than to live life
wondering what would've happened if I had tried.
— ALFRED LORD TENNYSON

Growth is painful. Change is painful. But nothing is as painful
as staying stuck somewhere you don't belong.
— MANDY HALE

Rising Above the Rut – breaking free from self-limitations, stepping out of your comfort zone, welcoming change, and discovering exciting opportunities for growth and success.

Congratulations, you're unstoppable! Another fist pump! Your toolkit is fully stocked, and you possess all the skills and personal qualities needed to live your dream life. You've made significant strides. You've examined your past, embraced the necessity of accepting it, and embarked on a journey of moving forward. You've revealed your passions, values and priorities. Your vision is clear and your roadmap, complete with well-defined goals, points straight to your desired destination.

You're taking consistent daily actions, achieving short-term milestones, and weaving purpose into your days, positively influencing others and rekindling joy and significance. Cherish these tools, master their use, and they will propel you to incredible achievements.

Rising above the rut involves harnessing not just your current circumstances, but your imagination as well. Are you summoning the courage to take the leap? Transforming any facet of life includes encountering risks and barriers, some predictable, others not so much. Yet, you possess the self-assurance to navigate either with grace. Your identity stems from your vision for the future, not from the weight of past hardships. Your focus shapes your reality.

Refuse to let hindrances or detours to morph into excuses for derailing your purposeful journey. While you can't control every external event, you're free to let go of what's not important, learn from every experience, adapt your course, and persist unwaveringly. The reins of your thoughts, emotions, and actions are firmly in your hands. No longer operating on autopilot, you're steering with intention, concentrating on today's accomplishments.

Confronted with challenges, remember that progress can be incremental, yet your desire to move ahead must remain resolute. Invest time in research to gain a deeper understanding of the requirements of your goals, and stay open to making course corrections. Each small step adds to your confidence bank.

Realizing your objectives and living your purpose necessitate casting off unhelpful habits, outdated convictions, self-imposed constraints, unwholesome connections, and other internal and external barriers that may have held you back in the past.

Excuses for procrastination are relics of the past. The negative internal dialogue has been replaced with positive thoughts and emotions. You've discarded the notion that a rut is your destined residence. Now, you consistently take action, even in the face of uncertainty about the route to your long-term aspirations. The steady belief in your capabilities fuels your journey.

You witness signs of progress unfolding before you. As you push past resistance, worry, doubt, and discomfort, you notice walls coming down and doors opening. Notably, when you make positive changes in one area, you observe improvements in other aspects of your life as well. Despite some steps not leading to the desired outcome, you never regret your efforts and experiences. The magic unfolds when you step into the unknown, take risks, and embrace uncertainty without any guarantees.

Your dedication is yielding results. Continue practicing and growing your skills, staying curious, and seeking opportunities. Invest in lifelong learning and don't hesitate to ask for help. Embrace self-love, be your own biggest supporter, and become a role model for others. Remember, people less qualified than you are already living their dreams, and now you have all the necessary tools to achieve yours too. Surround yourself with like-minded individuals pursuing similar paths; you'll discover inspiration and motivation there.

Maintain a healthy balance in your daily routine, ensuring you allocate time for work, self-care, self-improvement, and having fun. Trim away tasks that do not contribute to your dreams, freeing up precious moments to focus on what truly matters. Be mindful of your choices and make thoughtful and wise decisions. Hold yourself accountable by jotting down your daily goals each morning and reviewing your progress each evening.

You understand the importance of using a vision board or a vision book to create a vivid image of your current self and your desired future. You keep your before and after pictures in focus, engaging all your senses to mindfully experience the present moment.

Here are some simple suggestions for infusing your days with excitement and zest for life:

- Slow down.
- Appreciate life's simple pleasures.
- Foster and nurture relationships.
- Be self-sufficient.
- Stay curious and engage in lifelong learning.
- Concentrate on what makes you feel happy.
- Travel to distant places.
- Talk to strangers who seem very different from you.
- Exercise your five senses.
- Appreciate and use what you have—not what you wish you had.
- Assist others.
- Be clear on your goals and steps.
- Make decisions and act on opportunities, so you don't miss out on them.
- Practice general time management.
- Be spontaneous and allow for some flexibility.
- Be present and less focused on the past or future.
- Think more, listen more, talk less.
- Own up to your actions and outcomes.
- Keep your promises.

To continue experiencing joy, always have something new and challenging to work on. Remember, success is not about where you currently stand, but the direction you're moving toward. Express gratitude for the opportunities in front of you. In fact, make them your last thoughts before sleep and your first thoughts upon waking.

I hope you're finding the 3-Step Process valuable. Take your time to digest the guidance, practice it, and gradually apply it to improve various aspects of your life. This journey is yours so it's essential to follow your own roadmap at your own pace. Trust in yourself and relish the power of personal growth.

Allow me to remind you one more time: to be successful reaching your goals, you need to act on all three steps. It doesn't work if you skip one of them. Here they are again:

- Reveal your authentic *Purpose* by looking inward. Purpose is your reason for existence.
- Visualize where you want to go and create a *Plan* to guide your steps and decisions.
- Achieve consistent and meaningful *Progress*. Use your time and energy to foster a more fulfilling life.

In a nutshell: I recently read the book *Minimalism,* and it reminded me that we all have a unique vision of what we think will make our life feel meaningful. From modest beginnings, the authors soared as high-flying corporate money-managers, consistently earning more money every year, what many people refer to as living The American Dream.[47]

However, the big incomes, and even bigger expenses, did not fill them with passion or purpose. So, they sold off almost all of their possessions and became minimalists. They only held onto what they needed and focused, instead, on their health, relationships, passions, personal growth, and contributing to society. I am not an advocate for absolute minimalism, but the story reminded me of the importance of living in the moment and choosing our own vision for the future. You got this. Believe in yourself and ask, "Now what?"

As mentioned earlier, the 3-Step Process works wonders in essential parts of life like career, self-care, financial independence, relationships, lifestyle choices, and beyond. While I'll explore these areas more in the future, including on my

47 Joshua Fields, Ryan Nicodemus, *Minimalism,* 2011.

website, let's now focus on one of them. Let's review how this process functions in a significant life aspect: your midlife career, covered in the final bonus chapter.

JOURNAL PROMPTS

- Picture a scene from your ideal day and describe it using one sentence for each of your five senses.
- Compile a list of the thoughts that bring you the most joy.
- Identify two aspects of your life that you're eager to transform. Set aside the "how" and imagine unlimited possibilities. Pay attention to the emotions associated with these transformations.
- What are some obstacles and challenges you've experienced that you now feel grateful for, even though they were hard to appreciate at the time?

RECOMMENDED RESOURCES TO LEARN MORE ON THIS TOPIC

Book: *The Gift* by Edith Eger

Book: *Your Higher Self* by Stephen Warren

Video: *What is Your Purpose in Life* by Steve Harvey

Tip: Near the end of each day, ask yourself if you were better today than yesterday, and what you can do better tomorrow.

PART V

NOW WHAT?

32. USING THE 3-STEP PROCESS IN MIDLIFE CAREER

Work should bring value to others and meaning to you.
— MITCH ANTHONY

You are not your job. You are your work.
— TAM TAMASHIRO

Work – an activity involving mental or physical effort done in order to achieve a purpose or result.

Career – an occupation undertaken for a significant period of a person's life and with opportunities for progress.

Workism – a belief that work should dominate your identity and be your life's purpose; the life lived by a workaholic.

It's completely natural to ponder the importance and worth of the time we invest in our work over the course of years and decades. We ask ourselves, "Is this the best use of my time? Am I making a difference? Is this what I am best suited to do for the rest of my career?" Our work is a reflection of who we are. It's a window into our values, goals, and personality.

According to a Gallup report from 2013, only 30% of the U.S. workforce feels engaged in their work. People tend to form opinions or judge us based on our career choice and work effort. In this chapter we will look at using the 3-Step Process to find meaning and make the most of our prime working years. According to the United States Department of Labor, prime working years is defined as ages 25 to 54. I have also seen this referred to as midlife.

Work occupies a central role in many people's lives. We often hear that the experiences we face at work can significantly impact our wellbeing, either enhancing or hindering it. Many individuals hope that their work will not only bring financial rewards but also provide a sense of happiness and life satisfaction.

Discovering meaning in your work is vital for your overall mental and physical wellbeing. When your job aligns with your core values and beliefs, it ignites a deep sense of motivation and fulfillment within you. Engaging in rewarding work, that positively impacts us, drives our internal motivation and provides a sense of purpose and satisfaction.

As you practice mindful introspection, you may come to realize that your current work does not align with your values, passions, or abilities. I have spoken with many people who derive motivation solely from external factors, such as the paycheck, healthcare benefits, and paid time off. None of that is long-lasting motivation, so they soon feel frustration or even regret about their choice of career.

If this is your situation, it is a good time to step back and reassess your career—starting with the recognition that managing it is your responsibility. Too many people feel like victims in their careers, when in fact they have a substantial degree of control. I recommend they take a very personal look at how they define success in their heart of hearts and then find a path to get them there.

People often wonder if there is an age at which a sense of purpose in your work becomes less important. There is plenty of evidence that having a purpose is important throughout one's lifespan. So having a vision and making goals to achieve it is just as vital during your early work years as it is during midlife and beyond.

As we age and move through life, our purpose tends to change from one that is more self-oriented to one that is more prosocial or for the benefit of others. At any age, we all want to get out of bed in the morning and believe that today will be better than yesterday. Midlife is a period when numerous individuals conquer their fear of risk and opt to pursue a small business idea. Midlife is the perfect time to show up and have a positive impact on those around you.

Work can be used as an opportunity to enhance your social skills and confer dignity, self-respect, and pride. It also entails discipline, independence, and reliability, and is your contribution to society. Having a good attitude toward your work helps to deliver these benefits. These skills benefit you at every age.

If you want to get the most satisfaction from your work, choose a career that you will enjoy and feel passionate about and which you can learn to excel at. Strive to be the best at whatever work you choose to do. Increase your skill and grow your confidence. Authentic work can also be your greatest pleasure and help you achieve your life purpose. If you follow the 3-Step Process to learn who you are and what you want to become, create a plan to get there, and then take daily action to make progress, you will enjoy a successful career in alignment with your authentic self.

If I would have known and followed this as a freshman in college, I would not have chosen pharmacy as a major. Studying to become a pharmacist requires an enthusiasm for science skills. I always enjoyed business classes as its content felt more targeted toward my talents and interests. However, I chose pharmacy based on my mother's suggestion. We could have a long conversation about why I agreed to follow her advice, but I will leave that for another time.

Working as a pharmacist, you are responsible for verifying every prescription completed by your technicians, for accuracy and completeness. Just one oversight can result in injury or death to a patient. This expectation for perfection occurs in an environment loaded with distractions.

As you do your best to focus on checking each prescription, you are peppered with questions from the technicians to help solve a problem they are having. In addition, it is challenging to block out all the conversations happening between employees and customers.

Additionally, the pharmacist must answer customer questions, whether it's over the phone or while standing at the counter. The ability to focus on your work and manage these constant distractions is a key to your success as a pharmacist. Of course, over time, managing the stress leads to burnout.

The pace and stress of working in a pharmacy seem similar to working in a busy restaurant. The big difference, as I see it, is the consequence of making an error. In a restaurant you might get a poor tip or lose a customer. In pharmacy, you might find yourself in court, lose your job, or have your license to practice suspended or revoked.

Looking back now, I believe my personality, abilities, and interests were better suited for a career that involved working in an office and having private meetings with clients to discuss financial matters. However, I didn't have this book to guide me when I chose pharmacy. I hope you won't repeat the same mistake I made— or if you do, you'll have the tools to make a career change, just as I eventually did, even if it didn't turn out to be as a financial manager.

As discussed earlier, the Japanese concept of ikigai—your

reason for being—involves identifying the convergence of your personal passions, beliefs, values, and vocation. There are four components that must be met in order to achieve ikigai in your career. They are:

1. Are you doing an activity that you love?
2. Are you good at it?
3. Does the world need what you offer?
4. Can you get paid for doing it?

I have read about five dimensions of meaning in a career. You might want to re-number this list based on your personal priorities.

1. **Earning money:** You make your career decision based on earning power. How much income is needed to live comfortably and what careers might fulfill that?
2. **Achieving status:** Does your career provide you with the sense of pride and status you desire?
3. **Making a difference:** What does "making a difference" mean to you? Would a different job provide more fulfillment for you?
4. **Following your passions or interests:** Can you really do what you love these days? How have other people made a reasonable income out of their passions?
5. **Using your talents or skills:** When you are at your best, what are you doing? How can you find a job that allows you to do more of that?

If your current work doesn't give you feelings of happiness and satisfaction, you have a few options. You can choose to continue in your unsatisfying job due to self-doubt or fear of making a wrong decision. You can consider changing to a different career. You can learn to find value in your current role by changing how you think about your work. Or you could ask about a change of responsibility in an area that sounds more to your liking. Always stop to consider whether the problem lies in your attitude or mindset, rather than the job itself. If it's the former, then the wiser decision is to make an attitude adjustment, beginning with how you perceive your work.

Remember, you have the freedom to choose your attitude, mindset, and thoughts. Tell yourself that you want to do this and that you have the ability to do it successfully. Tell yourself you are committed to making it happen. Your positive thoughts will make you feel confident about what you're preparing to do, leading you to take action and make it happen. Once positive self-talk generates positive feelings, your next step is to create a plan and set goals.

If your opting for a career change, your plan should include a financial calculation to facilitate the transition. Also, include any necessary additional education or training, along with a realistic timeline to execute your plan. It's too important to approach it haphazardly; having a detailed plan is of utmost importance.

I know I'm not alone in realizing that my career wasn't fulfilling and making the decision to change. A career transition becomes more challenging when you have additional responsibilities, like children or financial obligations such as a mortgage, car payments, school loan payments, or moving expenses. Moreover, giving up healthcare insurance coverage from your current job can pose a risk. It's not a simple matter to let go of a stable income, even temporarily. However, a well-crafted plan has the potential to navigate these obstacles successfully.

Another idea you can consider before fully committing to a career change is to begin by finding a part-time job in the field you're interested in exploring. Sometimes, the other field might not turn out to be what you expected. Therefore, it's important not to burn any bridges as you navigate a transition to a more fulfilling career. Alternatively, you could initiate a small part-time business while still maintaining your current job. Seek out a gap in the market that aligns with your passion and skills.

One final career idea I recommend is to proactively write out a plan of what you would do if your job were eliminated six to twelve months from now. What preparations are necessary, and can you start making them now? It's always a good idea to have a backup plan in case of unexpected changes in your job situation. Consider if you would look for another job in the same line of work or use it as an opportunity to begin a different career. If it's a different career, include allocations in your plan for the time, energy, and money required.

In a nutshell: While work can provide a sense of fulfillment, it doesn't quite measure up to the lasting happiness you can experience through the close and intimate relationships you build with your family and close friends. Although, it's worth noting that the financial aspect of work may be appealing.

Whatever you choose to do for your work, it's important to stay prepared to take advantage of opportunity when it comes along. As you move along in your career, new doors may open. Or possibly, because of your new mindset and attitude, you realize you love what you are doing now. Perspective and plans can and do change.

JOURNAL PROMPTS

- What social conditioning have you received from your family and community, influencing your beliefs about what you should do and where you should go in life?
- Journal ten possible ideas, related to work, to push out of your comfort zone. This could be taking a class, asking for a new position within your company, networking, etc. Which idea seems easiest? Hardest?
- Journal ten work environments you'd love to experience and ten that you would absolutely hate. It could be a spacious office near the top of a skyscraper that has amazing views. Or a cozy art studio with large windows and plenty of natural light.

RECOMMENDED RESOURCES TO LEARN MORE ON THIS TOPIC

Book: *Do What You Are* by Paul Tieger, Barbara Barron, and Kelly Tieger

Book: *The Pathfinder* by Nicholas Lore

Video: *How to Find a Meaningful Job, or Find Purpose in the Job You Already Have* by Aaron Hurst

EPILOGUE

When you are young you have to fake wisdom.
When you are old you have to fake energy.
— SALMAN RUSHDIE

Rediscovering joy and purpose in your life is a remarkable achievement. I sincerely hope that you decide to begin implementing the 3-Step Process today. Delaying action will only result in feeling trapped in a cycle of stagnation. The significance of living a purposeful life rests in your hands alone. However, it's essential to acknowledge that opportunities may not present themselves again. The words of the Roman poet Horace, "carpe diem"—seize the day—emphasized the importance of living life to the fullest while you can.

Drawing from personal experience, I can attest that learning to alter your thoughts, emotions, and behaviors is no simple task. However, you'll swiftly recognize that it holds the power to bring about profound transformation in your life. The journey is gratifying and evolves into an anticipation of what lies ahead. Your small steps lead to big results.

Being present in the moment brings joy to your daily routine. Start your day with an open mindset and a positive attitude. Pause for a moment to relish the aroma of your first cup of coffee. Take the time to acknowledge the strides you're making in your relationships, self-care, and assistance to others. Focus on the positive aspects of your work. Everyone deserves to do something they love, an activity that gets them to jump out of bed and seize the day.

In your journal, write about the goals that ignite your excitement and how you can inspire hope within your friends, family, and community. Keep in mind that your purpose should extend beyond yourself to create a lasting, meaningful, and motivating impact. Taking action that is out of line with your purpose will not deliver long-term happiness.

To achieve your dreams and turn them into reality, you must engage in continuous learning and embrace growth through your mistakes. I suggest keeping this book readily accessible for moments of overwhelm or stagnation, providing you with a revitalizing resource. Remember, even the tiniest actions carry a sense of clarity, acting as a beacon to reignite your momentum and strengthen your dedication to turning your dream into a tangible achievement.

In a nutshell: The words in this book are only theoretical until you start envisioning how you can apply them to your life and change the way you think, feel, and act.

You have transformed into an empowered individual. The shackles of old fears, anger, and guilt have dissolved, making way for a motivated and confident new self. Your comfort zone has expanded, and every action, decision, and choice resonates with your life's purpose. You are actualizing your potential and broadening your horizons. What's the one thing you're working on today that's making you feel like a superhero?

REFERENCES

Man's Search for Meaning by Viktor E. Frankl

On The Meaning of Life by Will Durant (edited by John Little)

How to Write Non-fiction by Joanna Penn

"The Power of Purpose and Meaning in Life" by Lydia Denworth in *Psychology Today* – January 2019

What Brings Meaning and Purpose in Life? by Tyler J Vander-Weele in *Psychology Today* – January 2020

The Alchemist by Paulo Coelho

The film *Driveways* (2019) directed by Andrew Ahn

Finding Meaning & Purpose by Carol Vivyan on get selfhelp. co.uk

Find Your Purpose, Change Your Life by Carol Adrienne

Finding Meaning in the Second Half of Life by James Hollis

Netflix TV show – *After Life*

Lifescale: How to Live a More Creative, Productive, and Happy Life by Brian Solis

How Will You Measure Your Life? by Clayton Christensen

The Miracle Morning for Writers by Hal Elrod and Steve Scott

Sapiens: A Brief History of Humankind by Yuval Noah Harari

AARP The Magazine, "Happiness in Hard Times" by Sari Harrar (2020)

The Choice by Dr. Edith Eva Eger

Why Bother? By Jennifer Louden

The Rosie Project, The Rosie Effect by Graeme Simsion

Poverty Isn't a Lack of Character – TED Talk by Rutger Bregman

Question Everything: The Examined Life of Socrates by Ray Devine

Ponderings by Jonathan Pond, September 2020

"The Importance of Time Management" by Robert Ho in 2020 *Lifehack* article

Find Your Purpose in 15 Minutes by Julie Schooler

Blaze Your Own Trail by Rebekah Bastian

The Meaning of Life – A School of Life publication

It's Not All Downhill from Here by Terry McMillan

The How of Happiness by Sonja Lyubomirsky

The Power of Habit by Charles Duhigg

GOALS! by Brian Tracy

Live a Happier Life with a Free Mind by Fred Edwords

10% Happier by Dan Harris

The Purpose Effect by Dan Pontefract

The Happiness Project by Gretchen Rubin

Launch Your Career by Sean O'Keefe

Think Like a Monk by Jay Shetty

Burnout by Jill Lepore

There's a Name for the Blah You're Feeling by Adam Grant

The Things You Can See Only When You Slow Down by Haemin Sunim

Would I Lie to You? by Judi Ketteler

The Book on Storytelling by Michael Davis

Stressproof by Richard Sutton

The Walk by Richard Paul Evans

The Midnight Library by Matt Haig

"Scientific Method" by Regina Baily on ThoughtCo.com

Pursuit-of-happiness.org

What Is the Good Life? by Stephen Joseph

The Science of Happiness by Jose Ramos

Happy Money by Ken Honda

How to Create Healthy Habits – and Get them to Stick by Michelle Crouch

The Myths of Happiness by Sonja Lyubomirsky

Paths to Happiness by Edward Hoffman

Your Best Year Ever by Michael Hyatt

A Simple Five Step Process for Achieving Happiness by Ilene Strauss

Joy at Work by Marie Kondo and Scott Sonenshein

When I'm 65 – YouTube video produced and directed by Grace Raso

The New Retirementality by Mitch Anthony

The Richest Man in Babylon by George Clason

Keys to a Successful Retirement by Fritz Gilbert

Retirement Your Way by Gail McDonald and Marilyn Bushey

The Little Book of Common Sense Investing by John Bogle

Richer, Wiser, Happier by William Green

Fear of Falling: The Inner Life of the Middle Class by Barbara Ehrenreich

Confronting Capitalism by Philip Kotler

"Is Retirement Bad for Your Mental Health?" by David Ludden in *Psychology Today*

"What Will It Take for You to Age Successfully?" by Susan Krauss Whitbourne in *Psychology Today*

"Retirement Blues" in a Harvard Medical School blog post

One Small Step Can Change Your Life by Robert Maurer

YouTube video: *How Do I Get There from Here* by George Schofield

Ready to Retire? by Lyndsey Green

"How to be Physically and Emotionally Prepared When You Retire" by Dennis Damp – federalretirement.net

"Preparing Emotionally for Retirement" by AgeUK

"How Working on Your Goals Makes You Happy" by Norma Nikutowski in *On Happiness* blog

"Goal Progress and Happiness" by Timothy Pychyl in *Psychology Today*

"Some Early Childhood Experiences Shape Adult Life" by Maanvi Singh

Maybe You Should Talk to Someone by Lori Gottlieb

The Art of Self-Awareness by Patrick King

"You Are Not Your Thoughts" by Amber Murphy in *Declutter the Mind* blog

"Top 10 Reasons Why Education is Important" on uopeople.edu

Sacramento State University website – csus.edu

"The Why of Work" by Rodger Dean Duncan on forbes.com

Emotional Intelligence by Daniel Goleman

Wellsprings of Work by Samuel Halpern

"Working Longer May Benefit Your Health" by Christopher Farrell in *New York Times*

"Three Things to Take Care of When You Retire" by Liz Weston on Nerd Wallet

What Color is Your Parachute by Richard Bolles

The Adversity Hack by Meg Poag

The Latte Factor by David Bach

Are There Health Benefits to Staying in the Work Force Longer? by Christopher Farrell

The Meaning of Life Coffee Shop by Matt Tracy

How to Live Your Best Life by Kathleen Coxwell

The Retirement Crisis in America by DeWitt & Dunn Financial Services

"The Retirement Problem" from the *Knowledge at Wharton* journal.

"29 of the Most Important Values to Live By" by Barrie Davenport on liveboldandbloom.com

Winning at Retirement by Patrick Foley and Kristin Hillsley

The Last Lecture by Randy Pausch

What Now? by Ann Patchett

QBQ! The Question Behind the Question by John Miller

100 Ways to Motivate Yourself by Steve Chandler

"Know Thyself: How to Develop Self-Awareness" by Bill George on psychologytoday.com

Life on Purpose by Victor Strecher

Mindful Self-Discipline by Giovanni Dienstmann

"15 Ways to Build a Growth Mindset" by Tchiki Davis on psychologytoday.com

"A 67-Year-Old Who 'Un-Retired' Shares the Biggest Retirement Challenge 'That No One Talks About'" by George Jerjian in cnbc.com

Can't Buy Me Meaning? Money Cuts a Quicker Path to Happiness by Elizabeth Gilbert

Is Retirement Bad for Your Brain? TEDx talk by Ross Andel

Purpose and Self-Actualization: A Leader's Guide and Introspective Query by Mario Barrett

Soundtracks by Jon Acuff

Love Limitless podcast by Scott Miller

Retirement: A False Goal TEDx talk by Carol Black

Tightrope by Nicholas Kristof and Sheryl WuDunn

Ready to Pull the Retirement Trigger by Mary Sterk

Millennials Want to Retire at 50. How to Afford It Is Another Matter by Lisa Rabasca Roepe

"7 Core Qualities of Authentic People" by Stephen Joseph in *Psychology Today*

Destination Wellness by Annie Daly

How to Cultivate a Happier Retirement by NerdWallet

"Your 20s are Mostly Practice" by Cameron Albert-Deitch on CNBC

"What is the Sense of Agency and Why Does it Matter?" by James W Moore in *Frontiers in Psychology*

"What Is Mental Health?" on mentalhealth.gov

"Six Key Elements of Psychological Wellbeing" by Steve Race on the *Student Wellbeing Blog*

"What Are the Components of Mental Wellbeing" by Tanya Peterson in the *Mental Health Newsletter*

"Self-Reflection: Definition and How to Do It" by Tchiki Davis on berkelywellbeing.com

Life Is in the Transitions by Bruce Feiler

"A Low-Pressure Guide to Make Strength Training a Habit" by Danielle Friedman in *The New York Times*

"What Does It Mean to Be Proactive?" by Ashley Elizabeth on her Ashleyelizabethlynne.com blog

"Mental Health Definition" by Tanya Peterson in the *Mental Health Newsletter*

"The Relationship Between Mental and Physical Health" by Mandi Ryan on *Health & Wellness* website

"What is Psychological Wellbeing?" by Ivan Robertson on robertsoncooper.com

"How to Find Yor Reason for Waking Up in the Morning" by Eric Stewart on shiftthework.com blog

"15 Essential Ways to Practice Self-Reflection" on minimal-ismmadesimple.com

Discipline in Destiny by Ryan Holiday

Catapult Your Productivity by Damon Zahariades

"9 Self Limiting Beliefs That Are Holding You Back from Success" by Deb Johnstone on lifehack.org

"How to Take Charge of Your Life" by Mildred Newman and Bernard Berkowitz

Finding Your Element by Ken Robinson

The Purpose Handbook by Eloise Skinner

Live Your Dream by Joyce Chapman

Find and Live Your Authentic Dream by Lisa Hutterer on TEDx Cherry Creek

The Intentional Mind podcast by Angela Barnard

How Will You Measure Your Life by Clayton Christensen

"Personal Growth: Your Values, Your Life" by Jim Taylor on psychologytoday.com

"19 Life Purpose Examples to Find Your True Purpose" by Sarah Kristensen on happierhuman.com

Design Your Best Life podcast by Natasha and Richard Hazlett

"Time Management" from University of Georgia Extension

"What is Learning?" by Kendra Cherry on *Very Well Mind*

Changing Habits Changing Lives podcast by Azzy Aslam

"25 Good Habits for a Meaningful and Balanced Life" by Rachel Sharpe on declutterthemind.com

Breakthrough Goals by A.K. Spencer

"How to Commit, Achieve Excellence and Change Your Life" by Leon Ho on Lifehack.org

How to Change by Katy Milkman

The Magic of Thinking Big by David J. Schwartz

"Building Confidence and Self-Esteem" by Neel Burton in *Psychology Today*

The Magic of Believing by Claude M. Bristol

"What is Learning" by Kendra Cherry in *Very Well Mind*

Fearless by Rebecca Minkoff

Freely Determined by Kennon M. Sheldon

Predictably Irrational by Dan Ariely

"What Self-Awareness Really Is" by Tasha Eurich in the *Harvard Business Review*

The Resilient Mind on Apple Podcasts

Hidden Brain Podcasts with Shankar Vedantam

How to Unlock Your Greatness, Les Brown podcast

The Mountain Is You by Brianna Wiest

"The 9 Most Common Regrets People Have at the End of Life" by Grace Bluerock on MindBodyGreen.com

"12 Things People Regret the Most Before They Die" by Lolly Daskal on LollyDaskal.com

"How to Eliminate Fear" by Mel Robbins on *Resilient Mind* podcast

Change Your Paradigm, Change Your Life by Bob Proctor

Start: Punch Fear in the Face, Escape Average, and Do Work That Matters by Jon Acuff

How to Fight a Hydra by Josh Kaufman

The Power of Awareness by Neville Goddard

The Mental Game by Darrin Donnelly

Being the Best by Denis Waitley

Think and Grow Rich by Napoleon Hill

Minimalism by Ryan Nicodemus and Joshua Fields Millburn

ACKNOWLEDGEMENTS

I am deeply grateful for the support and encouragement of the many individuals who have contributed to the creation of this book. Your unwavering belief in the importance of this work has been a constant source of inspiration.

To all those who generously shared their stories, experiences, and insights, your willingness to open up and share your perspectives has greatly enriched the content of this book in immeasurable ways.

I extend my appreciation to the experts and researchers whose pioneering work laid the foundation for the ideas presented here. Your contributions have shaped the landscape of knowledge in this field.

I also want to acknowledge the friends and family who provided valuable emotional support and understanding throughout the process of writing and researching. Your presence in my life is a continuous source of strength.

Lastly, to the readers who embark on this journey of transformation, I extend my heartfelt gratitude. Your interest and engagement are truly appreciated, and I hope that this book offers meaningful insights and ignites further exploration.

ABOUT THE AUTHOR

Jay Nesbit resides in Cleveland, Ohio and holds a pharmacy degree from The Ohio State University, as well as an MBA from Texas A&M - Corpus Christi. Thriving in various pursuits and ventures, he enjoys investing in real estate and is the proprietor of his own publishing company. Jay's dedication also encompasses his role as a behavioral health pharmacist, managing medication to enhance the mental well-being of his clients.

During his leisure time, you can find Jay, a lifelong learner, exploring the latest arrivals at local libraries and bookstores, savoring a Cleveland Orchestra concert at Severance Hall, or immersing himself in new exhibits at the Cleveland Museum of Art. He derives immense joy from spending quality moments with his extended family, which includes four children and eleven grandchildren. Alongside his wife, Joyce, Jay cherishes their time together in the University Circle area of Cleveland, the winter months in St. Petersburg, Florida, and their attendance at the weekly summer programs at Chautauqua Institution in New York. Jay's passion for personal growth shines through as he fully embraces life's ongoing journey.

HAS THIS BOOK HELPED YOU TO RISE ABOVE THE RUT?

I would be incredibly grateful if you could take a moment to leave an honest review for my book on your favorite book review site. Your reviews play a vital role in helping other readers discover this book, and together, we can spread the message of breaking free from being stuck.

Thank you so much for your support.

To receive my complimentary monthly newsletter and learn even more about rediscovering joy and purpose in your life, kindly visit my website at:

WWW.JAYNESBIT.COM